SALESMANSHIP IN PRINT • VOLUME 2-24 D
AMERICAN WRITING PAPER COMPANY. G .

CW01652054

Publisher's Note

The book descriptions we ask booksellers to display prominently warn that this is an historic book with numerous typos or missing text; it is not indexed or illustrated.

The book was created using optical character recognition software. The software is 99 percent accurate if the book is in good condition. However, we do understand that even one percent can be an annoying number of typos! And sometimes all or part of a page may be missing from our copy of the book. Or the paper may be so discolored from age that it is difficult to read. We apologize and gratefully acknowledge Google's assistance.

After we re-typeset and design a book, the page numbers change so the old index and table of contents no longer work. Therefore, we often remove them; otherwise, please ignore them.

We carefully proof read any book that will sell enough copies to pay for the proof reader; unfortunately, many don't. For those we try to let customers download a free copy of the original typo-free book. Simply enter the barcode number from the back cover of the paperback in the Free Book form at www.RareBooksClub.com. You may also qualify for a free trial membership in our book club to download up to four books for free. Simply enter the barcode number from the back cover onto the membership form on our home page. The book club entitles you to select from more than a million books at no additional charge. Simply enter the title or subject onto the search form to find the books.

If you have any questions, could you please be so kind as to consult our Frequently Asked Questions page at www. RareBooksClub.com/faqs.cfm? You are also welcome to contact us there.

General Books LLC™, Memphis, USA, 2012.

A COURSE IN

WRITING PRINTED SALESMANSHIP 6' A COURSE IN SELLING PRINTED " SALESMANSHIP

THE concluding question in Lesson No. I was, "What is this thing labelled 'Advertising' that stands betwixt two salesmen?"

In that Lesson I also stated that I would tell you what "Advertising" as a whole is, and what it should be.

What advertising really is (generally speaking) can be gauged by sales tests (to which it does not, on the whole, ring true). "Advertising" as we know it, and on the Whole, fits the definition of "Hybrid" exactly. The second definition the Standard gives that term reads_as 'follows:

"Anything of heterogeneous origin or incongruous parts."

The biological meaning of the term, according to the same authority, is:

"A hybrid in which the blood has become enfeebled as the result of frequent crossings."

"Advertising" as generally practiced is not constitutionally strong; it lacks the rich red blood of salesmanship. This, then, is what advertising is.

I will now quote from one of my magazine articles:

In analyzing the sales problem of a great commercial institution some time back circumstances brought me in contact with its sales manager. The conversation very naturally hinged on advertising and I asked him what it was as he understood it.

"You," I said, "sell by the spoken word. I sell by the written word. Betwixt and between us is the thing called 'advertising'; what is it?"

He pondered a moment and then made answer:

"A sign, leading the buyer to the seller." I thought that a very good answer and told him so.

The precise sort of salesmanship that inheres in a sign ought to be quite obvious—it is limited and weak.

Yet ninety per cent of advertising falls under the definition this gentleman gave; note also that, in addition to being a sign only, its province as judged by a salesman is to lead the layer to the seller.

From which it appears that advertising of to-day is waiting on a buyers' market—— something I thought disappeared very shortly after war disappeared.

Interested in the-reactions of this sales manager to my subject, I stated:

"Most salesmen have an ill-concealed contempt for 'advertising.' For what reason? Is it not because they instinctively know that it does not possess the quality of salesmanship and strength of salesmanship that they know by personal experience must be injected into a situation in order to get profitable results out of it?" "Well " he answered, "I have found advertisin » g useful to me in selling."

"Of that I haven't the least doubt," I replied. "All advertising contains a certain amount of salesmanship and no advertising is so weak but what this diluted salesmanship may be found in it in some degree. You have found this modicum of use, and found that it has at least a tendency to help. To that extent you have found advertising useful to you; isn't that so?"

And to this he answered, "Yes."

It is quite important that it be grasped that advertising as generally practiced is nothing but a very weak form of negative salesmanship —it almost perfectly complies with the "enfeebled blood" definition of "Hybrid. " It would be practically impossible to construct or find any form of advertising that did not have some negative sales value to it. Consider this a moment and you will see it is true. Supposing I just buy white space, and maintain that regularly and run it regularly; it is just possible that a small proportion of people may ultimately become curious to know who buys and runs white space only; these people might write to the publishers of the paper just to satisfy themselves and in that way become acquainted with the advertiser, his name, his address, and his goods. Having got thus far some few might conceivably buy his goods. Manifestly the result could be traced to "advertising."

Assume another case: you buy paper; one day a man steps into your office, stands on his head, and then departs. The incident would furnish the day's bunch of jokes; if this were repeated for a week, or a month, you might, in curiosity, try to find out what the game was and as a result of your inquiry you might find the man represented a paper house; it is quite possible that you might manage to give him an order one day before he stood on his head — or after; you might even get into a fight with him and as a result of that fight eventually become friends and run quite a big account with his house — the outcome would be clearly traceable to the man's selling tactics. In other words, he could say that his abnormalities produced business and were therefore good sales tactics; they might be, and again, they might not be; the true measure of their value would be the profit and loss account.

A good deal of advertising is to-day, metaphorically speaking, standing on its head; it produces results and has at least a negative element of salesmanship, but, comparatively, it is diluted, weak, enfeebled; some salesmen find it of some use, while others, perceiving its very little use, despise it.

We now ought to be ready to grasp this working principle: "

We must measure the worth or worthlessness of advertising by the proportion of salesmanship inherent m it.

Unless you grasp this thought you will never be in a position to criticise advertising presented to you (and criticism, as we shall later see, is a very important element in business winning).

Unless you grasp this thought you will always be confuted by the man who will tell you that your criticism doesn't seem to be right inasmuch as the advertising has sold goods (or services).

Multiply puhlieity suflieiently and almost any kind of advertising will sell something.

As I Write I have a thermom-Th' S"i"g a"""Ph' 20 below zero to I20 above; in they hang in advertising

' ' ' ' sound advertising is to gister something In any kind of rcgismhigh-cmnd weather; it will never fail to do hizhmalwaysaimine M the perfect score as repre that. If we construct a sales sentedbytheioomark.

thermometer ranging from zero to IOO (the latter representing a perfect score) we shall find the sell_ ing atmosphere in which most goods or services function is practically never at zero; they hang in advertising around the IO mark; a negative salesmanship is there, but in experience it is very low. The aim of good, sound advertising is to register higher and higher, always aiming at the perfect score as represented by the hundred per cent mark.

Business is in business to sell goods (or services) at a profit; when business advertises it is trying to do that very thing. You must judge a piece of advertising matter therefore by its selling force; beauty, quality, typographical display, cost, etc., count for nothing if they do not help to sell at a profit.

Be careful to understand me here, however; art, beauty, color, quality, texture and typographical efiects are a distinct aid in selling if used aright. The mischief lies in using them wrongly. The sales thermometer, submerged in an "artistic" atmosphere, will not register at all—it will only respond to the proportion of salesmanship present.

You are shown an advertisement (in periodical, letter, booklet, or folder form as the case may be). You must judge it by salesmanship standards — nothing else. Unless you do this habitually you will never be able to discriminate between good and bad advertising. The advertisement is beautiful—but what of it? It is bizarre or novel— but what of it? It is ornate and costly—but what of it? It is of no use unless it sells; it grows in value as its selling atmosphere registers towards the IOO mark, and its measure of value is where it registers on the sales thermometer.

Unless you separate your artistic nature from your selling or commercial nature you will be in a continuous state of confusion or doubt in judging advertising; it is not necessarily a good advertisement if you consider it beautiful; it is not necessarily a good advertisement if you admire it; it is not necessarily a good advertisement if you are impressed with its cost; it is only good as it sells and the measure of its goodness is its sales strength.

I am trying to emphasize this sales point in your mind by every means in my power because everything else fails if you do not get this. The great majority of advertisers fail to understand' it; appa _ rently the great majority of advertising men fail to understand it also. Because this is so, advertising as generally practiced is almost invariably wrong; it is the great false premise of the advertising situation. Neither building norsituation can be built right on ifalse foundations. I earnestly hope, therefore, you will see the importance of judging advertising from one angle alone—the selling angle.

Artistry is one factor in advertising — one only. It has its place and it is an important place; it is as the frame to the picture, the casket to the jewel, the dress to the man; be careful in observing advertising that the frame is not presented for the picture, the casket for the jewel, the dress for the man ——-it is constantly done with disastrous effects. Advertising, in essence, is psychical, not physical.

Similarly, do not be misled in judging advertising by the cleverness of the text (except so far as it manifestly helps to sell). The witty paragraph, the clever pun, the literary skill may, in display, arouse your admiration, but are your haying instincts simultaneously aroused? If not, the announcement has simply missed fire; whatever else it may be it isn't a selling announcement, relatively speaking. It may make people laugh, it may make people cry, it may make people smile and it may do any one of many things, but if it doesn't have the urge to huy it is worthless as an advertisement, however valuable it may be to art, or wit, or literature.

Again, do not misunderstand me; the arts of literature are of great service in writing advertising; with them one can point a selling moral or adorn a selling tale; advertising can draw on all art and science with profit to itself and all concerned. But it must draw right. The test of advertising is sales strength. Literary or artistic strength without sales strength is useless. A man advertising must aim primarily at sales—not at art. He must aim at sales—not literary eficect. He must aim at sales — not typographical effect. He can bring all these things in to help sales and:

They are useful as they add to prqfit and useless as they suhtraet from it.

Now if this is clear the art of studying and handling advertising ought to be clear; it is fundamental and simple—it is a selling proposition throughout and a good advertisement (in periodical, letter, booklet or other form) becomes nothing more nor less than a salesman.

Sound advertising is printed salesmanship.

The art of writing printed salesmanship is the art this Course endeavors to teach.

Business men as a rule do not appreciate the fact that advertising is in effect printed salesmanship. The term "advertising" has simply confused them. Questioned, they think it stands for something, though they hardly know what. As a consequence a great deal of confusion has prevailed; primarily men have lacked a standard or measure with which to judge advertising. A beautiful advertisement has been thought a good advertisement. A clever advertisement has been thought a good advertisement. A costly adver tisement has been thought a good advertisement. A witty advertisement has been thought a good advertisement. Men have been judging advertisements by and through widely different emotions and not by the single standard of sales force.

Because of this also men constructing advertisements have begun their work from wrong angles in different conceptions, and on foundations of varied and differing kinds. The objective of some has been artistry, the objective of others wit, the objective of others literature; some have dressed, some have scintillated, some have talked. All, however, have been presenting BUSINESS, whose sole object is to make sales at a profit.

Business knows that some advertising has made sales at a profit and it has gone after similar experiences, utilizing the thing termed "advertising" in doing so, and business has come to know that "advertising" has been both resultful and resultless in such varying degree that it has appeared to be nothing more nor less than a game of risk or chance. This condition has arisen because business has never clearly defined "advertising" (simply multiplied salesmanship or salesmanship multiplied), nor have the men who have furnished advertising to business. The man owning the business in all probability looks at adver tising from one angle; the man writing the advertising for the business in all probability looks at it from another angle; the owner may be literary, and the "writer" artistic; each may quarrel with the work and views of the other as expressed in "advertising" unless they mutually understand the province of advertising, which is to make sales at a pro/it and which, as a consequence, must be printed salesmanship, and which, furthermore, must be graded high to produce the best and most lasting results in sales and goodwill, because when all is said and done the house' that made sales through representatives standing on their heads is not the house that would produce the best and most lasting kind of an impression.

Is this clear? Sound advertising should be nothing more nor less than printed salesmanship graded high by the standards of salesmanship. If that is correct a great deal of confusion about the subject must necessarily disappear; advertising will gain immeasurably in efifectiveness because, as we proceed, it will become manifest that we can ascertain where each unit grades by clearly defined tests and rules founded on bedrock principles from which there can be no variance and, as a consequence, no dispute.

It will, of course, be understood that the art of written salesmanship difiers from the art of verhal salesmanship and that the processes of one as a consequence differ from the processes of the other. That, of course, will be clearly explained as we proceed. We are now getting our bearings, as it were, defining and understanding what we are talking about —— silhouetting our subject prior to attacking details.

And now a final word: America is a great business nation; an enormous sum is spent on advertising already, though the art is but in embryo; a very large proportion of advertising done is an economic waste, capable of almost indefinite improvement; the field in action is enormous; yet a stupendously larger latent field exists because all business men are in business to sell goods or services at a profit over cost, and all business men are eager to utilize any force that will demonstrably aid them in an eflort to which the major part of their lives is devoted.

Imagine, then, the field waiting to develop to definite, positive, scientific standards.

All men do not want to do business on a national scale, but all business men want to do business on some scale that will give them a commensurate reward for the time and effort they give to it; therefore all men in business are legitimate "prospects" for a legitimate advertising-selling service such as PRINTED SALESMANSHIP can give to them.

As we proceed we shall. deal with periodical advertising (newspapers and magazines) quite extensively, although this by no means implies that you are to be carried into that field; quite the contrary, in fact; we shall see, however, that what we learn there applies intensely, concretely and specifically to the class of advertising you are more familiar with, i. e. Direct Mail as represented in fac-simile letters, folders, broadsides, booklets, house organs, signs, posters, etc., etc. These, of course, will be taken up definitely in proper order and sequence. We shall find as a matter of fact that all printed salesmanship is related— that principles applied in periodical advertising apply with equal force in Direct advertising, and that factors which adversely affect periodical advertising also adversely affect and handicap Direct advertising. Our principles, therefore, will embrace the whole field and will be found adaptable and applicable to any and all advertising situations.

If in this Lesson we have gained a better understanding of the thing we are talking about, we are a long way ahead.

THE GENERAL SERVICE DEPARTMENT AMERICAN WRITING PAPER COMPANY JOSEPH A. BORDEN, DIRECTOR
lo SOUTH LA SALLE STREET, CHICAGO, ILL.
PUBLISHERS

A COURSE IN WRITING PRINTED SALESMANSHIP 5-' A COURSE IN SELLING PRINTED SALESMANSHIP

Lesson-7(0). 3

From

DEPARTMENT or GENERAL SERVICE AMERICAN WRITING PAPER CO. Jos. A. Borden, Director

Q Sou-rn LA SALLE STREET

CHICAGO

PRINTED SALESMANSHIP 5' A COURSE IN SELLING PRINTED SALESMANSHIP

Wri'tten Sxelusively for U. T. vi. Trinters BY
ROBERT RUXTON

THE GENERAL SERVICE DEPARTMENT

AMERICAN WRITING PAPER COMPANY JOSEPH A. BORDEN, DIRECTOR
10 SOUTH LA SALLE STREET, CHICAGO, ILL.
PUBLISHERS

A COURSE IN WRITING PRINTED SALESMANSHIP 6- A COURSE IN SELLING PRINTED SALESMANSHIP

T will be recollected that in Lesson No. I we defined the term "Stimulus. " In Lesson No. 2 it was stated that sound advertising is nothing more nor less than printed salesmanship. The main idea embodied in that Lesson is the necessity of singleness of purpose and attitude in writing or examining advertising; that will be gained if we iudge the worth or worthlessness of each announcement by the intensity of the sales stimulus it eontains. Please always remember that. An advertisement may be beautiful, it may be witty, it may reflect literary art and skill and it may be full of sales stimulation——that would be a IOO per cent announcement; again, it may be beautiful, it may be witty, it may reflect literary art and skill, and it may be very deficient in sales stimulation —— that would be a 5 or IO per cent advertisement. We will, of course, presently go into salesmanship and find out what it is — ATTENTION, INTEREST, DESIRE and AcT1oN merely represent the sequence or order in which it functions. At present, if you will think of advertising as selling you cannot go far wrong. When you examine an advertisement ask if it is a selling talk; when you construct an advertisement make it a selling announcement. In both cases the urge to buy must be clearly perceivable to you (not necessarily to the "prospect, " however).

The way to fashion sound advertising is to endeavor to put IOO per cent sales stimulus in the message, totally irrespective of anything else— then put IOO per cent additional into the things that carry the message.

Always consider the message first; write it first; have that right; afterwards, consider the other things; if you work that way you will never be guilty of preparing a strong ATTENTIONgetter, but a weakIN"ri:1u-:sT-, DESIRE-and ACTIONgetter.

An advertisement is a psychical, not a physical thing; art in efiect simply ornaments it; get the man first; then clothe him. Start with the psychical and finish with the physical.

We will now review a few advertisements as a kind of preliminary study in the art of writing printed salesmanship.

You will recollect the definition of advertising given by a sales manager in Lesson No. 2, i. e., "A sign, leading the buyer to the seller." Let us see if we can find a few advertisements strictly conforming to this definition. The following are taken from car signs: these announcements with suitability and exactitude—they have no sales urge at all—-if a man wants to hay they lead him to a place where he can be served.

At that it would probably be all right if a very big "If" did not constitute an upsetting factor—If there were not COMPETITION. A competitor with a buying urge in his advertisement would win over the "sign" practically every time.

One man announces he has pearls and jewels for sale — he is, of course, surrounded by hundreds with similar commodities for sale. Another announces he handles Montclair real estate —-so, no doubt, do a few active local competitors. Another group announce they are in the real estate business in New York—as are several thousand others. The Virginian Railway has transportation to sell — to those wanting to buy it. Two theatres present two plays—to those who want to see them the announcement of time and place is no doubt a convenience.

In the New Orpheum we find a variation from type; a little salesmanship creeps in in the words "Presentation de Luxe." The Rialto also embodies a little salesmanship in the words "Foremost pictures—Music. Beautiful. TenseThrilling——Appealing." These adjectives may sway a man at the last moment, diverting him from a competitive show.

It ought to be clear enough that a little study of these announcements would result in a big injection of salesmanship. This of course would increase their efiectiveness — their " pull" — their results. The space would cost no more.

One slovenly farmer will get IO bushels of corn from an acre of land — another will get 6o bushels — the space in a newspaper, letter or booklet can be cultivated in the same degree.

Now read the Postum advertisement;

here is a man who has cultivated his space—it is full of salesmanship.

Now understand that advertisements I to I2 inclusive will probably be effective to some degree; if they do not sell they at least index by a public sign and this fact (publicity) gives even the poor advertiser an advantage (sometimes a very big advantage) over thevman who doesn't advertise at all.

It is quite possible for such advertisements to show a profit over their cost through the multiplying or magnifying power of publicity, but it will be perceived, I hope, that if they were better advertisements they would achieve better results.

If you criticised one of these advertisements, you would perhaps be confounded by the statement that it "pulled. " The answer to that is: if it "pulled" with that sort of copy it would pull infinitely better with copy that had the sales urge in it.

Inventors of the steam engine were satisfied when it went —— but straightway arose another army of inventors dissatisfied till it went better. Civilization did not rest satisfied because the first steamboat crossed the ocean——it went on per. fecting steamboats till they cross the ocean far better, and are quicker and safer.

Advertising is a very young science—Rowell of Printers' I nk saw its beginnings with the beginning of his business life and it is as imperfect today as was the first railroad train, the first steamboat or the first dynamo; indeed, the conceptions of the men who lead advertising today are like the conceptions of the men who led in the time of Galileo—-all wrong. Galileo put them right but was condemned to death as a consequence, nevertheless his truths live while their fallacies died. Physicians before the time of Harvey were practicing without knowledge of a vital fact — blood circulation. Harvey set them right but was reviled for doing so — but his truth lives while their fallacies died.

As Galileo and Harvey needed (and found) interpreters and apostles of the truths they found, so advertising needs them; it is due for evolution or revolution and the printers of America have a wonderful opportunity to grasp and preach a new and true advertising creed, to their own personal betterment and the infinite betterment of advertising.

Below is an "indexical" or "Sign" announcement occupying a modest inch of space.

DENTIST
Permanently Located
265 Sprntly Bldg.
Cor. Tazewell and Granby Sh.
Telephones — Office, 24909—Residence 26792

No. 16

If (preserving the message intact) you put this in a page of space you gain ATTENTION value because, all other things remaining equal, the eye will go to larger rather than to smaller things.

While a larger number of people will read the message, if enlarged, the sales value of the message has not been altered in any respect (outside of the multiplication of readers).

Now a great many advertisers are trying to substitute ATTENTION value for sales value, putting what is in effect an inch message in 36 inches of space.

An advertisement so treated is disproportioned, and, as a consequence, wrong. A selling announcement has four aalanced parts in ATTENT1oN—IN— T1-ziu-:sT—D1-:s1 1u:—AcT1oN, and if one is dominant and overshadows the others an essential proportion has been violated and,inevitably,itwill not "work" as it should. This point should be carefully noted because one of the great abuses and mistakes oftoday's advertising is the substitution ofATTENT1oN values for other vital elements ofthe selling act.

In the INTERWOVEN announcement, for instance, ATTENTION VALUE is strong but SALES VALUE is very weak. The artist is manifestly to the front —— but where is the salesman? This advertisement occupied a page in a great national weekly and a page in that publication costs $7,000 per issue. This particular advertisement, being in color, costs $8,500 per issue. I recently commented on this in a magazine article as follows: _

A comparison is invited between the Cooper,

Wells & Co.'s sock advertisement (No. I8) and the "Interwoven" sock advertisement.... Cooper-Wells illustrate their "Iron Clad" sock completely, and par-_ ticularly illustrate the vital part their process protects against wear. The text supports the illustration, and the illustration supports the text.... The advertisement, therefore, has a strong sales appeal —much more so in my judgment than the page advertisement of the "Interwoven " people.

The "Interwoven" announcement is a very good example of an advertisement strong in Attention value but weak in all other sales elements of 'Interest, Desire and Action. "No equal for wear" is a generality. The barest hint of any characteristic feature in the sock is conveyed in the term "Interwoven." Toe and heel are concealed in the illustration (though I should assume they are vital parts to figure). One instinctively follows the man's hand to the end of his fingers to discover——what? Neither illustration nor copy conveys an adequate message.

In the "Interwoven" announcement, in other words, the artist has worked to gain ATTENTION. He certainly registered there. In the CooperWells announcement, on the other hand, the artist has not only worked to gain attention but he has also worked to make the sale. Here the artist-salesman and the writer-salesman have worked in unison and the result has been a selling announcement.

(T 0 be continued)

A COURSE IN WRITING PRINTED SALESMANSHIP 69 A COURSE IN SELLING PRINTED SALESMANSHIP

Lesson 4

From

DEPARTMENT or GENERAL SERVICE

AMERICAN WRITING PAPER CO. Jos. A. Borden, Director lo SouTH LA SALLE STREET

CHICAGO

AMERICAN WRITING PAPER COMPANY

JOSEPH A. BORDEN, DIRECTOR
Io SOUTH LA SALLE STREET, CHICAGO, ILL.
PUBLISHERS
A COURSE IN WRITING PRINTED SALESMANSHIP 6- A COURSE IN SELLING PRINTED SALESMANSHIP

"Forcibly presenting itself to the mind or attention; presenting a remarkable appearance; notable or impressive; as, a striking aspect."

Watch for situations in advertising that may be described as striking, because striking impressions are responsible for great advertising mischief. A striking object naturally attracts the eye and focusses the ATTENT1oN, and every business man feels glad _when something that will attract the eye and focus the attention of thousands on his business announcement is presented to him. He will very likely buy that striking thing, be it border, illustration, sketch or something else.

Yet ATTENT1oN is but one-fourth of sound advertising. This great fact needs all the emphasis that can be brought to bear to make it clear. I seek to reach a certain destination by car; I need the automobile, the engine, the gas and the oil; if one of these factors is lacking I cannot go; I do not gain much if the body of the automobile is presented to me without the engine, yet that is what happens when an advertisement is practically all ATTENTION — a striking thing.

Suppose I am crossing a morass on horseback and can make four hard places in four leaps of the horse. If the animal leaps to the first and finds the second has disappeared overnight the task of reaching the third is beyond him.

If one link is removed from the selling chain it is no longer a "pulling" instrument. A few crude illustrations will perhaps serve to make this clearer:

In sketch No. I

We see a "prospect" approaching a commodity or service that he is to reach by an easy climb up the rungs of shopping or by mail efibrt. Each stave is placed at a normal height for his climb and he will not have much difficulty in reaching his objective.
, on sznvicz
T

But supposing (as in No. 2) he climbs to the first rung of ATTENTION and finds the rung of INTEREST missing? He is very apt to give the matter up without further consideration. (This isn't absolute, however—we will discuss that point later.) No.2 _ that ofDEs1RE missing!
that he finds the rungs " "
of ATTENT1oN and INTEREST in place but
ATTENTION, INTEREST and DESIRE, but finds the Ac-
TION rung missing!

Now we will look at No. 6. Here a "possibility" is strolling around and indifferently or vaguely knows of the commodity or service. The rung of ATTENTION is missing, however, and without it he cannot even begin his climb.

Now psychology, physics, law, and all else rightfully place tremendous importance on a beginning, a start, a commencement and an impulse or initial momentum.

"What's well begun is half done," said Horace. The law maxim reads, "The principal part of everything is the beginning." " Begin," said Ausonius; "to begin is half the work. Let half still remain; again begin this, and thou wilt have finished."

ATTENTION, then, is the beginning and the beginning is of very great importance —of such great importance that men give it overbalancing importance in advertising; they fee-dA'rTENT1oN but starve INTER1:sT-DEsIRE-AcTIoN.

That is the great foundational mistake and error which advertising is making. All rungs in the climb to the commodity or service must be strong and sturdy or the average man will not use them.

In looking at sketches (I to 6) we see there is an upright or pole supporting the rungs; if the rung of ATTENTION is missing the "Possibility" will hardly trouble to climb at all; he may be hardly conscious of the existence of the thing as he passes it; he might experience little or no urge to go higher than INTEREST if the rungof DESIRE be missing (sketch No. 3), but if he got firmly planted on the runglof DESIRE (sketch No. 4) he might be roused enough to climb the pole even if the rung of AcTIoN were missing.

Something like this happens indeed in many advertisements that "pull" despite the lack of one or more of the selling elements; the reader supplies them out of his own mind ———reeonstructs the advertisement, as it were, and shinnies up the pole.

Every missing rung, however, eliminates people who would otherwise climb. An advertisement strong in ATTENTION value but weakin INTEREST

DESIRE-ACTION values has three points of elimination, and if these losses could be seen advertisers would be staggered at their enormity.

ATTENTION, while one of the most important rungs of the sales ladder from one standpoint, is also one of the weakest from another standpoint. The urge at ATTENTION is very low; it strengthens.at INTEREST, and becomes intense at Diasnu-:nine men out of ten will not take to the pole at ATTI-:NTIoN, but a very large proportion of the ten would take to the pole at DESIRE..

What madness then to coax to the ATTI-:NT1oN rung and leave the rungs of INTEREST—DESIRE—AC'I'ION far out of reach! '

Now the fact is that the message is one thing (psychical) and art is another (physical). They must be rigorously separated in your mind when criticising advertising or constructing advertising. The artist is a powerful ATTENTION-gCtt6l'. Let him deliver, within his province, IOO per cent ATTENTION value if he can. With him let the message deliver IOO per cent ATTENTION value if it can. Let the artist keep to his own sphere, and the Writer-salesman to his. Construct the message first——let art strengthen it afterwards if it can.

Some of the great mistakes committed in advertising arise through the artist absorbing space to such an extent that the salesman has no room.

Some of the greatest mistakes committed in advertising arise through allowing the artist to write the message.

Ordinarily the artist is no more a salesman than the salesman is an artist.

Advertising is selling; nearly all selling is consummated by words. Syllables govern the world. The province of the physical is to dress and minister to the psychical; the spirit of things is clothed with the substance of things; mind utilizes matter; matter does not utilize mind. We will go into these things more exhaustively as we proceed; at present I wish to follow my ATTENTIONIN-TEREST-DESIRE-ACTION illustrations with actual examples of advertising that conform. In the reproduced announcements I have indicated the various " zones ':

In

"1, WONDERFUL BOOK—resd about ltl A Tells how eanlv Stones and Plays are conceived. Wflllffl. "riveted. sold. How many who don'! DREA they can write. suddenlv lind it out How the Scenario Kings and the '_ SKOFY Queens live and work. How bright men ' sad women. without any specihl experience I--arn to their own amazement that their sirn plell ideas maylun-nah brilliant plotslor Plays '_.1 ml Stones. How one sown Imagination may '_ provide so endless (old-mine 0! Ideas that lvY'i.'lI HIDDY Success and Handsome Cash -Royalties. How new writers get their names l'il0 print. How to tell ll you ARE s vmter How to develop vow "story lancy," weave clever word-pictures and unique. thrilling. How your friends um be your wont judges. Hoe: tellutu plots _

to avoid discouragement and the pi ails oi Failure. How Io mu!

This surprising book is sbwlulely rec. No charge. No obliggion Your copy is svlllllll for vou. rite (or It now. lust addre-

ISS RUTH _. WOLCOTT, of Wixonsin, is one of scores of men and women who easily earn the extra money they need to buy Christmas presents for their j relatives and friends by helping us to take care of the holiday demand for The Saturday Evening Post, The ' l Ladies' Home journaland The Coun try Gentleman.

"Considering the time I, spend," she writes, "I make more with Curtis work than I do with any other work I have tried. My largest order last year was for Christmas gift subscriptions."

During the next two months, thousands upon thousands of gift subscription orders will be placed for our three publications. Some workers will receive generous profits for forwarding such orders. Who will earn this money in your neighborhood? Why not you?

Attention-

Interest-

Desire-

/fction.

/fttention Zone.

Interest

Zone.

Desire

Zone.

fiction Zone.

AVE you ever considered ' why our richest men come from our poorest _ boys? Isn't it a strange thing that it is almost invariably a young fellow who starts life without 5 cent in the world. without education, without influential friends—-in short, without one si e solitary advantag&who aurumulates mi ions of dollars? Isn't it a miracle that inside of a comparatively few _years s man can rise from abject poverty to fabulous wealth?

Astonishing. certain —-but more important. it is wonderfully inspiring. or it means that no man need be held down by circumstances. Once ho knows the "millIonaire's secret." he an put it into operation regardless of all obstacles. His fancied handirapa simply yantsh into thin air. He suddenly finds that eve lhllll he louches turns to gold—money flows in upon nn-—forQtme showers him with its favors. Every! ll!' he wants weems to come to him just as surely and easily as day comes alter night.

Cflooss Between Lou Pay and Magnificent Earnings

This vcrv minute you may be face to face with your BIG opportunity—_vour one chance to earn the biggest money of your life! Right now your decision may mean the dificrenm between a life of plodding, routine work at low pay and a career of inspiring success and magnificent earnings.

for now you are oflered the very opportunity that has made other men rich. that has brought them more money than they ever dreamed of earning.

It is the same opportunity that lifted Warren Hartlo of Hill N. Robcy 51.. Chicago. out of a yob In the railway mallarrs-ice. where in trn years he had never Rotten heyond ll.6(XJ a year. and landed him in n ll0,000 a at b. It jumped Charles Berry of Winterset, lows. from a month as a farmhand. to ILGJO a month. It brought to C. W. Campbell. of Grcenshurg. Pa.. a clerk on the railroad. a position that paid him ll.Mi III thirty has.

These men and hundreds more have found their lg Opportunity in the wonderful field ol Saleunanship. They are all Master Salesman now. They are rn-rning the ' 'est money of their lives-—rnore than they ever thong t poasbl¢—t hey are engaged in the most lllflfllllhi work -in the world—thcy are independent. come and go as they pleue—they meet big men—every minute of t.ha day istilk-d Illh lhflllllfl' variety.

Your BI Opportunit may be here too. in the wonder field of Sa sinanship. erha you say u have never even thought of berotnin a ut before you decide one way or the ot,esainine the facts for your self. See what Salesmanshi oflers you—why ll is the best paid of all vocations—w y thera is no limit to what you may earn. Read the amazing proof that no matter what you are dblhl now. you can quickly become a Mastrr Salesman in yous spare time at homr.—read how the National Solesmeifs Trainsn Association in its nation-wide search for men to fil the peat need for salesmen. has devised a wonderful system that reveals to you every Secret of Selling. See how this famous OITIIIIIIIIOII helps you to a good position In the lino ol Se ling you are best filled for.

The opportunity that the N. S. T. A. olers you Isa ho your one chance to earn the b' st mooe ol your Iife, as It has been for hundreds others. ut whglgvgf you do. don'! pass it by without gutting the fang.

No. 13 $200 sixsms 0718.

Sell us your spare time. You should easily make each hour bring you an extra dollar. Spores ofspati l'e-tiEme representatweso T/eSa1ur a_y vmin

Interest Post, T/xc Ladies' Hume Yaumal and

Zone The Counlry Gen/leman will earn

' more than $200.00 before Christmas.

Why not you too' It costs you but

a 2c stamp to learn all about our lans. Experience IS unnecessary.

-rofits begin at once just clip off De-"re- the coupon and mail It today

The perfect advertisement, like the perfect man, is an illusive quest; few of these advertisements are perfect, nevertheless they exhibit in characteristic degree the principle of construction that should always rule in preparing advertisements, letters, booklets, broadsides, folders, etc., etc.

Preserve these advertisements carefully, because, later, we shall probably review them from different advertising-selling angles and apply tests to them other than those of order and sequence.

Incidentally the Standard's definition of ATTENTION may now interest, i. e. —

"The direction of the mental powers to a specific object,... especially when vigorous, voluntary, and concentrated."

And of INTEREST!

"3. Pedagogy. The efibrt of attention on the part of the pupil encouraged by the endeavor of the teacher to make his subject attractive."

At present the full definitions are not given but it will be observed that ATTENTION and INTEREST are almost synonymous with the Standard. In reality they blend very closely — almost imperceptibly. ATTENTION may be gained for a flash of time but INTEREST holds it; to my mind, therefore, INTEREST would seem to be in eflect SUSTAINED ATTENTION.

AMERICAN WRITING PAPER COMPANY

_ JOSEPH A. BORDEN, mREc'roR

IO sovrn LA SALLE sTREET, CHICAGO, 1LL.

PUBLISHERS

Need makes the naked man run. —French Proverb.

Gain has a pleasant odor, come whence it will. —Portugue:e Proverb.

ADVANTAGE. Any position, state, circumstance, or the like, favorable to success, progress, health, or other desirable condition or end. — Standard Dictionary.

POTENTIAL. Possible but not actual. A possibility. — Standard Dictionary.

A COURSE IN WRITING PRINTED SALESMANSHIP 6-' A COURSE IN SELLING PRINTED A SALESMANSHIP

THE importance of salesmanship in copy has been heavily emphasized in prior lessons as the fundamental and primary thing in advertising; it might now be as well to try to discover what salesmanship is; or, in other words, try to find out the elements of which it is composed.

It should first be understood that there are two kinds of salesmanship; the first (true salesmanship) is positive and creates an order that, otherwise, would not be procured.

The second is negative and takes an order.

In a negative condition of salesmanship eonditions have "sold" the potential buyer to such effect that he either waits for a salesman or sends for a salesman.

Conditions can "sell" a man as efiectively as the best salesman can — sometimes more so.

When, for instance, a storekeeper finds an insistent demand on him for a brand of goods he some time previously refused to stock, he is extremely likely to be "sold" on that brand even though no salesman comes near him.

To put it in cruder terms, famine may "sell " people bread, thirst "sell" them water, and necessity, or semi-necessity, "sell" them anything. A "salesman" takes such orders.

In a population of a hundred million people there are always conditions working to ' 'sell " people certain things. A man may become convinced that he wants real estate, a youth that he wants a gun, a mother that she wants a baby carriage, etc., and these people are "sold" by the negative form of salesmanship that takes their order, or really "distributes" to them, just as the Red Cross might hand out loaves of bread in a famine.

A "salesman," under such conditions, need not have much selling aaility when he comes face to face with the potential buyer. Conditions have put that buyer very eflectively through the four stages of Attention-Interest-Desire-Action.

In an accentuation of necessity we can easily conceive of " prospects " chasing " salesmen." This happened very often indeed in the late war. It is happening all the time in a constantly changing circle.

You have no doubt heard it stated that, if a salesman will really work eight hours a day, day after day, making a steady system of calls, he will do business, no matter how poor a salesman he is; and you have perhaps also heard that a man out of work will certainly land a job if he keeps calling and asking, hour after hour, day after day.

There is a lot of truth in that, too: The Law of flverage begins to work for the constant "plugger," to the end that, while he cannot sell (positively speaking), he will "sell" (negatively speaking) by finding someone eventually who wants to buy.

Such a man's problem (he does n't always realize it) is simply to canvass a sufiieient number of people. This, you will see, is very similar to "Sign" advertising, spoken of in Lesson 2 and illustrated in Lesson 3. Such advertisements, by virtue of circulation, "call" upon a great mass of people and (by the Law of Average) find some who want to buy.

Briefly put, we may say that the negative "salesman" works extensively, while the positive salesman works intensively. "Sign" advertisements, put in a medium of small circulation, would hardly pay their way; put into a medium of large circulation, they may pay their way. The Law of Average gets to work as numbers are covered.

It may here be understood how and why an "advertisement" that would not pay under normal conditions of circulation may pay under abnormal conditions of circulation. In other words, an advertisement that could not hope to pay in a medium of, say, 1oo,ooo circulation (being phrased negatively, and partaking of the "sign" character) might pay in a medium of two million circulation; indeed, the tendency of the "sign" type of advertisers (negative copy) is to drift to the relatively few media of great circulation (when such advertisers are wealthy) because there, . One of the principles of advertising-selling we will endeavor to cover as these Lessons proceed.
and only there, do they find such results as they are led to expect advertising can deliver, and there, and largely there, you will find the "sign" type of advertising one would expect to find.

"Sign" (negative) advertisers are indeed, as a rule, to be found either in mediums of very large circulation or of very small circulation. The first have the wealth necessary to carry them into the great white light of publicity that (sometimes) brings them their expected profits, while the second, lacking that wealth, assume "advertising" is not much good anyhow and advertise chiefly to "support" some struggling publication or as a means of contributing to some charity.

Both types are living a negative advertising life. The wealthier advertiser would get infinitely greater results if he changed from negative to positive "copy," and the smaller "advertiser" in making the same change would discover that publicity of the right kind had wonderful selling possibilities.

N considering selling it should be further underl stood that while PRINTED SALESMANSHIP is similar to ORAL SALESMANSHIP in a great many respects, it is dissimilar to it in a great many other respects. We cannot inject into PRINTED SALESMANSHIP, for instance, that human element called "Personality," nor can we adapt a written salesmanship appeal to individual or to peculiar conditions as a salesman can;we can, however, oflset these disadvantages by other advantages and thus even up the score.

As we proceed we shall see that WRITTEN SALESMANSHIP is one force, and oral salesmanship another. We shall see that they work in harmony, however, and get the maximum of results when united.

We can now proceed to discuss PRINTED SALESMANSHIP. I would personally outline it as follows:

Written salesmanship shows the potential buyer an advantage through positive, moving words that attractively demonstrate the advisability of seizing such advantage.

Written salesmanship shows a gain that it is an incentive to take.

The parallel with oral salesmanship will, of course, be noted because we only buy to gain something (real or fancied, as the case may be), and the salesman who could not show us some gain of some kind or character would not get very far with us.

Now what is salesmanship? We have in prior lessons seen the form or shape in which it works (Attention-Interest-Desire-Action), but that, metaphorically speaking, is only the shape or form of the brick and not the substance of the brick itself, and as we must know the substante of Hereafter, unless otherwise stated, it will be understood that I refer to WRITTEN salesmanship when I use the term "salesmanship." ' bricks before we can manufacture them, so also must we know the substance of salesmanship before we can manufacture it.

Now "salesmanship" is a complex term, and when we meet anything complex we can only get to understand it by taking it to pieces either physically (as with hammer, screw-driver and wrench) or mentally, through questions.

For instance, if you know little or nothing of an automobile and I drive one up in front of your home and ask you to come and look at it, I am showing you in the object designated by the term "automobile" a very complex thing; if you want to know all about it, it will do very little good for me to show you the engine, and gas, and oil, and battery and tell you that those are the things that make it go. In doing that (as in telling you that ATTENTION-INTEREST-DESIRE-ACTION make a sale go),I am giving you a very limited outline of the entire mechanism, and if you were very anxious to find out the principles that made the machine go, you would open up the hood, for instance, and say, "What is this, and what is that?" and "What does this do, and what does that do, and how and why does it do it?" and before we got through I might have to take you to an automobile school where we could take that machine to pieces before you, show you the parts, and how they worked, put them together again, and then let you drive the machine yourself.

This might be tedious and tiresome, yet it would be necessary. We have to go to the minutiae of things before we can learn about them; we learn the alphabet before we can read, and arithmetic before we do algebra.

You will recollect the reply of the ancient teacher to the impatient king: "There is no royal road to learning"— king and peasant have to plod along the road of detail and study, so if you want to know the art of salesmanship, the art the whole world wants, you must do the same. We will therefore begin by defining the terms used in my outline or definition, and if you will follow them and bear with them for a little while I can assure you we shall soon come to more interesting and less studious details.

First, please note that the entire definition of "Salesmanship" hinges on the term "Snow." Let us begin there, then, and find Where it leads us.

"SHOW. I. To cause to be SEEN; present to view; exhibit; Ex1osE; (2) To cause to be UNDERSTOOD or known; present to the intelligence; EXPLAIN; reveal; tell; as, to show a Way; (3) To cause to see or understand; guide; convince, as, I will show you; (4) To cause to be accepted by the JUDGMENT; make evident by LOGICAL processes; PRovE; DEMoNs'rRATE."

You see what a lot there is in that simple little term "show "— more perhaps than you realize —-yet as you may see if you will continue to follow where it leads by continuing to define its terms in turn.

In all definitions, unless otherwise stated, the Standard Dictionary is the authority used.

Let us, for illustration, take a part of the definition of:

“DEMONSTRATE. To derive from admitted premises by steps of REASONING which admit of no doubt; Pnovr: indubitably, as to demonstrate a proposition. Speeif., to TEACH by exhibition of examples; to point out; show; indicate; MAKE CLEAR.”

Now note:

“DEMONSTRATOR. One who proves or dem onstrates in a CONVINCING and conclusive manner. One who exhibits or explains something or some process, as a TEACHER. Speeif. , one who shows the parts of a... structure anatomically DISSECTED; as, a demonstrator in operative dentistry or of anatomy; (2) A SALESMAN who exhibits to customers the operation and possibilities of a machine or process."

Note carefully how, in defining from “SHow" to “DEMoNsTRAToR,” we come eventually to SALESMAN.

As indeed we must. You may have your own personal ideas about a salesman, and have perhaps considered him a well dressed, prosperouslooking individual who talked well and told good humorous yarns entertainingly— and indeed a salesman may have all those attributes (which correspond to interest in presentation) — but you will find if you observe further that the good salesman has something deeper than those things, and that he practices them, not in every sales talk, but in such sales talks as demand them.

You will find, for instance, that a good salesman is also: (1) A LOGICIAN.

(2) A TEACHER. (3) A DEMONSTRATOR. (4) AN ’ANALYsT.

Now a salesman may not know he is these things because many salesmen get their results unconsciously or subconsciously; they could not tell you how they get them; their ignorance of the how, however, does not alter the how, and in a difiicult sale if you will watch the salesman you will see him utilize principles of logic, principles of teaching, principles of demonstrating and principles of analysis and synthesis.

Let us, for instance, pause on the term:

“DISSECT. (I) To cut apart or to pieces; divide into portions; especially to separate the parts of... in order to examine the structure; anatomize. (2) To ANALYZE and examine CRITICALLY; discuss or examine in detail; as, to dissect a defence or a writing...; or as, the dissection of an argument.”

Note how closely the definition of “ANALYs1s” dovetails: “ANALYSIS. The resolution of a compound into its PARTs or elements. The act of ascertaining, separating or unfolding in order the elements of a complex body, substance or treatise.”

So you see logic, language, definitions, say that

‘an ANALYST is in effect a DEMONSTRATOR, ia demonstrator is in effect a SALESMAN, andva salesman is in effect a man that SHOWS-—- 3.

’ need.

And don’t overlook “CRITICAL.” A synonym of “criticise" is “Examine,” which means:

"To inspect or scrutinize...; investigate critically as to composition, condition, character, or the like, for the purpose of arriving at a conclusion, ascertaining a fact or the truth, etc.... To test as to composition or qualities; as, say, ANALYZE.”

So you see a salesman under many circumstances will also be a CRITIc; in observing this chain we get this truth:

Logic, teaching, demonstrating, analyzing and criticizing, help the sale, are concomitants of the sale, and very vital and necessary parts of the sale.

A printing establishment that I represented made its sales through three main departments, named, respectively:
(I) Department of Constructive Criticism.
(2) Department of Analysis and Plan.
(3) Department of Continuous Supervisory Service.

Sales contracts in these departments, ranging from $250 to $1,000, rested absolutely on factors of logic, teaching, demonstrating, analyzing and criticizing; these then being the‘factors of the sale, constituted, in essence, PRINTED SALESMANSHIP because 90 per cent of the sales of this establishment were made through and by THE PRINTED WoRD.

Nothing but Analysis-Plan in constant motion.

Reason is mistress and queen of all things. —Cicero.

There is nothing I know of so sublime as a fact. — George Canning.

Truth is tough. It will not break, like a bubble, at a touch; nay, you may kick it about all day, like a football, and it will be round and full at evening. — O. W. Holmes.

A writer who builds his arguments upon facts is not easily to be confuted. He is not to be answered by general assertions or general reproaches. He may want eloquence to amuse or persuade; but, speaking truth, he must always convince. —— _/unius.

Passion and emotion themselves are, in us, not without thought, and may always be treated as thought in a glow. — Martineau.

A COURSE IN WRITING PRINTED SALESMANSHIP 6’ A COURSE IN SELLING PRINTED SALESMANSHIP ’

N Lesson 5 a working outline or definition of PRINTED SALESMANSHIP was given as follows:

“Written salesmanship shows the potential buyer an advantage through positive, moving words that attractively demonstrate the advisability of seizing such advantage. “ Written salesmanship shows a gain that it is an incentive to take.”

In that Lesson We defined the terms “Show” and “Demonstrate” together with related terms that they led us to. VVe have still a few words or terms to define in the above, one being:

"POSITIVE. That is, or may be, directly AFFIRMED. Real; actual; existing. (4) Laid down or uttered by positive authority. (5) Not admitting of doubt or denial; incontestable; undeniable; certain; sure; as, proof positive. THAT WHICH Is CAPABLE or BEING DIRECTLY AND CERTAINLY AFFIRMED/'

Now note "PosITIvIsM": I do not necessarily quote full definitions, but only such parts as serve to make points clear. _Full definitions will be found in Standard Dictionary—my authority in every case unless otherwise stated.

"A way of thinking that aims at and accepts only such propositions as are positive, as distinguished from speculative, and are based upon ascertainable facts.

"3. Certitude, or the claim of certitude in knowledge."

Presently we shall see that the good personal salesman is under many conditions a PosITIvIsT (limiting the term to business experiences, of course). "Posl'rlvl'rY" in fact means:

"Exactness in the scientific determination and statement of (business) phenomena."

And what does "EXACT" mean? "Accurately or precisely conceived or expressed; characterized by definite knowledge or principles; strictly observant of accuracy, as, ' "Abraham Lincoln... was so exact in all his deal ings that people called him HONEST Abe."'

And now let us get an illustration of "HoNEsT" as follows (from Standard):

"One who is honest in the highest sense is scrupu lously careful to adhere to all known TRUTH and right even in thought."

Now we are getting down to one of the great fundamentals of either written or oral salesmanship because our chain of definitions leads to "Truth."

Note these two illustrations:

"The mind takes oflense at every phenomenon of both inner and outer experience which appears to

"The Hindus'... very word for truth is full of meaning.... Truth... was with them simply that which is." — Max Miiller, "India Lect."

The two quotations above go to the very foundations of advertising psychology, which we will realize as we progress, but it will be sufiicient now if the reader carefully notes that the good salesman (written or oral)

Thinks and acts in terms of positivism, and is a business positivist simply because he is exact, honest, and truthful.

WI-IY he is this the Lotz and Muller quotations hint at and we will discuss more fully as we proceed; it will be sufiicient to note here that we are discussing the sum of the qualities that make up a good salesman, and, as a consequence, when we have them all, correctly grouped, we have Salesmanship.

N definition of W_RITTEN SALESMANSHIP we said:

"Positive, MovING words." Let us now get definitions of "Move" and "Moving" as follows: "MOVE.... 2. To incite to an action, as by per suasion or representation; cause to act; influence; prompt; as, he was moved to help. 3. To stir to deep feeling; excite the sympathies or emotions of....
9. To make progress or advance; speei/'. , to progress in a certain manner. Mus. ,To PROGRESS FROM ONE PITCH TO ANOTHER. To incline toward.

"MOVE, n.... (2) AN Ac-r IN THE CARRYING OUT or A PLAN; A STEP TOWARD AN OBJECT; as, a clever move.

"MOVING. I. CAUSING TO MovE; IMPELLING TO AcT; INFLUENCING; INSTIGATING; PERsUADINo."

As, in salesmanship, one moves the prospect through specified zones of thought, i. e., ATTENTIoN-INTEREsT-DEs_IRE-AcTIoN, the relation of this term to salesmanship and its great significance in salesmanship should be plainly apparent.

It will be seen also that we have been led to a new term —"PERsUAsION"; we shall nearly all recognize persuasion as a selling force and we nearly all know that good salesmen are persuasive; that term, however, has dif¥erent facets, and lights, and meanings, so we should have its definition:

"PERSUADE. To win to a purpose or course by entreaty, eloquence or REAsoN1No, or by an appeal to feeling, passion, or sELF—INTEREST; induce to do or to refrain from an act; influence by MoTIvEs."

Persuasion and conviction are practically synonymous in WRITTEN SALESMANSHIP, though they may not be in the ordinary relations of life; "Persuasion" in its "entreaty" or "passion" sense implies the influence of a person well known, and therefore the influence of personality, friendship, or blood-relationship. In the personality sense persuasion is seldom used in WRITTEN SALESMANsHIPthough it may be, of course, when one friend writes to another, the subject being a sale of some kind. PERsUAsIoN in the sense of WRITTEN SALESMANSHIP means an urge on the facts adduced. I want to make that clear because there is a school of writers in business who urge emotional (largely persuasive) pleas, in lieu of reasoning or demonstrating pleas. If these men thought out their position logically they would discover that there is no emotion that does not base on a reason. I touch on this now briefly in connection with the definition as above, and we will go into it more fully as we proceed.

Such persuasion as there is in business presentation must come after the facts — not before them. Maria Edgeworth in Moral Tales brings out the correct order and sequence as follows:

"To convince is my object. If it were in my power I should,upon the present occasion, disdain to persuade."

"Persuade" in the emotional sense, and an appeal to the feelings in a persuasive sense, would be indicated where a friend in adangerous situation appealed (either passively or actively) to another for aid. In such case a major reason for not rendering such aid might be completely fiouted or defied; a similar thing might happen and a man act against his judgment if his sweetheart appealed to him to follow a certain course of action for the love he bore her. It is seldom that one gets such powerful leverages in selling, so, in selling, persuasion on the whole must vest in facts and on facts, and this is particularly so in impersonal PRINTED SALESMANSHIP. An oral salesman may have' knowledge of certain domestic or personal relationships that would move the "prospect" and he might judiciously utilize these as an "emotional" appeal, and win a sale through them, but purely "emotional" situations in PRINTED SALESMANSHIP are rare, and, even when found, must be used carefully if an anti-climax is not to be risked.

"Emotional" copy may inhere in charitable appeals, some political situations, etc., because there will be found a background of religion, sympathies, patriotism, etc., that is urging with the writer, but these are special situations, seldom found in merchandising services or goods. As the Standard says:

"Persuasion is so largely dependent upon conviction that it is commonly held to be the orator's work first to convince in order that he may persuade."

The rhetorical definition of "Persuade" is also instructive:

"The department of invention in which the object is to move the will, in order to lead to a new choice or course of conduct. It embraces (I) PERSUASION PRQPER, in which motives are presented to lead the heater to the direct formation of a positive purpose, and (2) DIssUAsIoN, in which the object is to change some dominant purpose."

Persuasion in an emotional sense is sometimes available in business presentation, therefore it should not be excluded, but is properly included in our definition of "MovINo"; yet it should be remembered that persuasive force in written salesmanship will largely inhere in the introduction of a reasoned motive, or motives.

We find the term "Motive" in illustrations of " Persuade, " which we got, in turn, from definitions of "Moving," all therefore being embraced or related in the original definition of salesmanship in print, and I have asked you to follow the chain step by step in order that you ma.y be convinced that the definition is comprehensive enough, embracing enough, and sound enough to be ADGPTED as a working formula, so that when you begin to write PRINTED SALESMANSHIP you will keep that formula of thirty-three words before you as a compass or guide, and thus get to the point you should reach without deviation or confusion.

N our final rhetorical definition you will see that we got "Motive," which relates to "Moving," as will be readily seen:

"MOTIVE. Having power to move; tending to move; causing motion. That which causes or tends to cause motion, or to incite to change or to action; moving or impelling force, whether in a literal or figurative sense. Ethics. That which acts as an inducement to preference or choice; that which, speaking figuratively, tends to move the will'; a strong or impelling influence towards some particular Ob_Ct to be obtained or end to be secured."

When a salesman shows an ADVANTAGE he also automatically shows a NEED or a LACK. When he shows a need or a lack he creates, as it were, a mental vaeuum into which mind, as air, tends to rush and fill. A good salesman, in the final analysis, by giving the "prospect" a motive or series of motives, really causes said "prospect" to buy. A synonym of "Motive" is "Reason," and reason upon fact,-and fact upon demonstration, within the rightful limits of the subject, provide the incentive for the "prospect" to seize that which is offered.

And "Seize, " when its definition is examined, is seen to be allied to Action (the final phase of salesmanship) in the fact that it:

"Catches or takes hold of suddenly" in its physical sense, or grasps or "seizes an idea" in its figurative sense.

HAVE said, "A good salesman really CAUSES I a 'prospect' to buy." That is true in a very literal sense. I have seen a (comparatively) poor salesman "C1. osE" (get the order) at a great expenditure of personal energy, and in forms and Ways that clearly showed.the pressure he was bringing on the "prospect" to make him buy.

The man I speak of was a life insurance salesman whom I had frequent opportunity to watch while selling. His deficiency lay in the fact that he did not usually work his "prospect" adequately through the "Desire" stage (he was good at Attention-Interest); consequently, when CLOSING TIME came (Action) the "prospect" would hesitate and demur. Here the salesman used to unscrupulously utilize the force ofa strong personality and literally overpower the other man. The sales made were, as a consequence, not true sales since many _men, after signing the applicat1on and paying the money, regretted the transaction the moment this salesman left them. He knew this, and provided against the rebound by getting the cash with the signature; nevertheless the sale was not a satisfactory one as a large percentage of that kind of business "lapses. "

A good many men would call that salesman a "good" salesman, and he was, in the sense that he earned fairly good money in insurance work. He had the faculty of getting the Attention of his "prospect" and of sustaining it after he got it (Interest) and he had the mesmeric or hypnotic faculty offoreing the "prospect" over Desire into the "Action" stage; the looker-on could always tell when he had decided to "close" the "prospect" and clearly perceive the "forcing" tactics he was adopting to the discomfiture of said "prospect." Discomfiture is the correct word, because the "prospect" felt he was being made to do a thing that, at heart, he was unwilling to do and that he would rid himself of eventually (by a prompt lapse).

Now that is n't a true sale.

That insurance salesman dealt on an average in premium payments ranging from $25.00 to $250.00, those figures representing the boundaries of his customary sales.

Now I have seen sales made where the figures ranged from $250 to $1,000 in which there was no "forcing" action at all and in which, apparently, there was no "closing" action even (if the formality of taking a check voluntarily handed over by the prospect and giving a receipt for it be eliminated).

In other words, the "prospect" bought. He did n't buy because conditions had "sold" him but because he had been "sold" by a salesman who had caused him to sell himself.

These sales that I speak of were made sometimes by PRINTED SALESMANSHIP alone, and sometimes by a combination of PRINTED and ORAI. salesmanship.

These were true sales. A lack had been shown. A need had been silhouetted, an advantage had been indicated and a-MoTIvE given to which the "prospect's" mind MovED like air to a vacuum, irresistibly, but naturally, without force, friction or discomfiture, because in the words of Beecher:

"God made man to go by motives."

And

"He will not go without them, any more than a boat without steam, or a balloon without gas."

And what is a synonym of "Motive"?. Don't forget... "REAsoN"; here it is:

" REASON. I. That which is supposed or aflirmed to support or justify any conclusion, belief, or PLAN or AcTIoN; a fact, truth, or end to be attained, which serves the mind as a rational ground or MoTIvE; proof for an opinion, judgment, or resolution."

"God made man to go by motives" — by reasons —— by facts —— by truths — indeed he did; those are the motivating forces of humanity and you get outside of them and within a fallacious circle the moment you try to substitute other things for them such as art, color, typography, "striking effects," etc., etc. , — these are not motivating forces, but simply dress for motivating forces, and if you have n't got reasons, facts, proofs and truths in your "copy" in proper sequence and effect, it won't go, never will go, and never can be made to go.

And so, through a long but true circle sounded link by link,we come back toour original definition:

"Written salesmanship shows the potential buyer an advantage through positive, moving words that attractively demonstrate the advisability of seizing such advantage.

"Written salesmanship shows a gain that it is an incentive to take."

THE GENERAL SERVICE DEPARTMENT

AMERICAN WRITING PAPER COMPANY JOSEPH A. BORDEN, DIRECTOR
I0 SOUTH LA SALLE STREET, CHICAGO, ILL.
PUBLISHERS

PRINTED SALESMANSHIP E3' A COURSE IN SELLING PRINTED SALESMANSHIP

Wri'tten gxelnsively for U. T. e/1. 'Printers BY
ROBERT RUXTON

THE GENERAL SERVICE DEPARTMENT

AMERICAN WRITING PAPER COMPANY JOSEPH A. BORDEN, DIRECTOR
IO SOUTH LA SALLE STREET, CHICAGO, ILL.
PUBLISHERS

Self-love and reason to one end aspire.

—Pope. Self-love, the spring of motion, acts the soul; Reason's comparing balance rules the whole.

Man, but for that, no action could attend, And, but for this, were active to no end. — Pope.

That the principle of self-love (or, in other words, the desire for happiness) is neither an object of approbation nor of blame, is 'sufficiently obvious. It is inseparable from the nature of man as a rational and a sensitive being.

— Dugald Stewart.

Self-love is a due care for one's own happiness and well-being, which is perfectly compatible with justice, generosity, or benevolence toward others; Selfishness limits endeavor to a narrow circle of intensely personal aims, destroys all tender sympathies, and is ultimately fatal not only to the welfare but to the happiness of him who cherishes it. — Standard Dictionary.

It is manifest that self-love is in human nature a superior principle to passion.... so that if we will act conformably to man's nature, reasonable self-love must govern.— Bishop Butler's "Sermons."

A COURSE IN WRITING PRINTED SALESMANSHIP 6- A COURSE IN SELLING PRINTED SALESMANSHIP

ELF-LOVE rules human nature as gravity rules S the universe, and when this is perceived it will be further perceived that it is human nature to utilize an advantage when shown.

Note the definition of "Advantage" and ask yourself if you would ordinarily renounce an opportunity for betterment so offered:

"ADVANTAGE. — (I) Any position, state, circumstance, or the like, favorable to success, progress, health, or other desirable condition or end; superiority, as in position or place;. a favoring circumstance; that which conduces to one's benefit or gain; profit; improvement; in ethical use, that which concerns oneself or one's personal interest.

"SYNoNYMs: Ascendency, benefit, blessing, boon, gain, privilege, profit, service, success, superiority, utility, vantage. To use (any condition or circumstance)as a means of profit, of progress, or of effecting one's purposes. "

You may, it is true, refuse a seeming advantage, but you would hardly refuse that which your best judgment and reason told you was a true advantage.

Now, many things (commodities or service) offered for sale have a true advantage for the potential buyer, and such potential buyers may abound in great numbers; yet the thing offered does not sell as well as it should.

Assuming that potential buyers are being reached in sufi-iciently large numbers, or, in other words, assuming that the advertiser (periodical or mail, as the case may be) is in his market, offering his wares, there can be but one answer to such a condition — the advertiser is not showing his advantage as he should. When he does, buying, like gravity, will function.

We can cut at the trunk of a tree till we think it ought to fall, but if we have n't cut far enough and deep enough the resistance of the wood fibres will defy the pull of gravity and the tree w0n't fall; we would be very foolish if we said we had engaged in the act of cutting down a tree, and, because the tree would n't fall, we had found the act of cutting down trees would n't make trees fall. If we were wise, we would perceive that when we cut far enough and deep enough the tree had to fall in conformity with a law of nature.

Potential buyers of an advantageous thing must reach the buying stage if they cut far enough and deep enough.

I said "Must." It is as certain as the rush of air to a vacuum; as certain as the attraction of gravitation; if a thing won't lift up (in response to applied strength), we look for the reason, and, if we look far enough, we inevitably find it; if a thing won't fall or roll down when we have apparently cleared the way for it to do so, we again look for the reason and just as inevitably find it when we look far enough and deep enough.

When a thing truly advantageous to potential buyers isn't bought on the presentation made, look for the reason; it's there, and will inevitably be found if you look far enough and deep enough. As a matter of fact, almost always the reason why a thing does n't sell is because the reason why the potential buyer should buy is lacking, or is weak.

The o osite of "weak" is "stron." Let us PP g define both terms:

"WEAK. Lacking in power or force. Lacking in mental or moral strength.' Deficient in power or vigor of intellect; liable to err or fail through feebleness of conception; foolish; silly; showing poor judgment or want of discretion; as a weak plan; a weak decision. Deficient, as an instrument or part, in strength, force or efficiency. Insufficiently resisting stress. Ineffectual, as from deficient supply or other reason. Inadequately furnished or supplied, as in.
some given particular; as, the enemy was weak in ships; lacking in eflective power or potency. Defective in stimulating or other properties of its class; of less than customary strength and potency; Nor WELL SusTAINED BY FAcTs, REASON 011 CONscIENcE; as a weak argument; a weak pretext, a weak title. Wanting in vigor, impressiveness or interest; as a weak book, There may, of course, be other reasons outside of "copy" and these are found under ANALYSIS, a factor we shall treat later. a weak drama; a weak style. Lacking in influence, energy or authority."

And now:

"STRONG. Having great mental or moral force; imbued with effective abilities or aggressive in principles; forcible; moving or acting with a high degree of force; STRoNo ARoUMENTs OR PRooF. Marked by boldness or vigor of execution; as, a strong literary style; graphicness in delineation; made or constituted firmly or solidly; not easily overthrown or altered; exhibiting unusual enthusiasm or interest; deeply earnest; zealous; as, a strong temperance advocate; characterized by intensity in degree; to take a position that can be defended with strong arguments; hold or assert a claim, belief or opinion in its full force."

Note the relation to "Positive" and "Positivism"-I "POSITIVE. That is, or may be, directly AFFIRMED; real; actual; existing. Laid down or uttered by positive authority. Not admitting of doubt or denial; incontestable; undeniable; certain; sure; as proof positive. THAT Wrncn Is CAPABLE 0F BEING DIRECTLY AND CERTAINLY AFFIRMED."

Now, one important element of strength in copy is a positive way of treating and stating it. It must as a consequence rest on authority and truth and fact and evidence. That way you work on and govern mind, which is the very foundation of things.

Note the sweep of "Mind" as defined by the Standard:

"(I) An abstract, collective term for all forms of conscious intelligence, or for the subject of all conscious states; the entire psychical being of man.... The intellect or REAsoN in its normal condition; sanity."

Now, the vital point here is to approach a proposed presentation from the positive angle; to be sure that it is-given the positive facets; to be certain that it will reflect positive lights; to know that it will be impregnated with positive thought, citations, and illustrations.

In approaching a presentation you have to ask yourself in effect:

"How can I explain this thing?
"How can I prove this thing?
"How can I teach this thing?
"How can I reason this thing out?
"How can I demonstrate it?"

For, understand, there are different angles or facets to every subject; you may have to explain a technical product (or term) to a non-technical public. You may have to prove a thing to a skeptical public. You may be under the necessity of literally teaching that public. If physical demonstration cannot be achieved (by nature of the subject), you may have to demonstrate mentally (by a process of reasoning), and if the thing is capable of being so handled and exhibited, you may demonstrate it with drawings and pictures.

All these angles of presentation fall under our original term "Snow." The Missourian with "You've got to show me" is an inciter to salesmanship. His readiness to act when shown is an incentive to salesmanship, and his favorable action after being shown is proof that you have achieved salesmanship.

N our definition of "PosITIvE" we struck the term "AFFIRM," and as it has an important bearing on advertising procedure we had best define it here:

"AFFIRM. To declare or 'state POSITIVELY; make (a statement) and maintain it to be true; declare to be a fact; aver, as to aflrm one's innocence.

"./Zfirm has less of egotism than assert (as seen in the word sch'-assertion). It has more solemnity than declare, and more composure and dignity than asseverate which is to assert excitedly. In legal usage, aflirm has a general agreement with depose and testify," it differs from swear in not invoking the name of God. 2. An afiirmer, in law, one who testifies under judicial affirmation instead of formal oath."

The final lines of our "PosITIvE" definition bring out the point Iwish to emphasize In regard to "AFFIRM": '

That which is capaole of being directly and certainly afiirmed.

Afiirmation does not produce the proof with its declaration or statement but rests on, or springs from, that proof.

"ASSERTION. A positive declaration, especially when unsupported.

"'We have seen strong assertions without proof."' funius' Letters.

"To assert without proof is always to lay oneself open to the suspicion of having no proof to offer, and seems to arrogate too much to one's personal authority, and hence in such cases both the verb assert and its noun assertion have an unfavorable sense; we say a mere assertion, a bare assertion, his unsupported assertion; he asserted his innocence has less force than he afirmed or maintained his innocence. /fssert has always a controversial sense, resisting or challenging opposition.... Almost any criminal will assert his innocence; the honest man will seldom lack means to vindicate his integrity: _

"'(This) would need some better proof than bare assertion to make it believed.' "

Hamilton': "Metaphysics."

We have seen that periodical space is very expensive (from $4,000 to $7,000 per page) and that this expense automatically limits space.

In limited space proof cannot be consummated as it should be, so the message in lieu of presenting proof is aflirmative in character, and proflers it in the form ofa booklet that will be sent on request.

An emphatic advertisement in brief space, unsupported by obtainable booklets or other media, is essentially assertive, not alone in character but also in efleet.

"Strong assertions without proof" are to be seen in all magazines or other periodicals and in action provoke statements very similar to that of Hamilton:

" (This) would need some better proof than bare assertion to make it believed."

The reader may dishelieve, or he may simply remain skeptical; the mere definition of those two terms will show in each event a very undesirable frame of mind:

"DISBELIEF. A conviction that a statement... is untrue. DISBELIEVE. — To refuse to believe, give no credence to; to hold to be false.

"SKEPTICAL. Requiring more proof. Incredulous; distrustful; as, he was skeptical of the result."

And:

"INCREDULITY. A withholding or refusal of belief; indisposition to believe.

"'A story so startling was received with outcries of incredulity.' " — FROUDE. " The English in Ireland."

AND what is proof? Let us go to the Standard once more and ascertain what this essential thing is, in all its bearings and all its facets, as it applies to PRINTED SALESMANSHIP:

"PROOF. The act or process of proving, in any sense. Speeifi, the establishment of a fact by EVIDENCE, or a truth by other truths. (2) A trial of strength or excellence; a test; as, the proof of a musket. (3) The amount or degree of evidence that convinces or is suited to convince the mind of the certainty of truth or fact; evidence and argument sufiicient to induce belief; as, the proof of any charge or statement; proofs of devotion.

"The essence of logical proof consists in so combining propositions which we know, that we finally see some other proposition to be a necessary admission, which was not seen as such before."

B. P. Bowne's "Studies in Theism." "4. Law. Anything that serves to convince the mind of the truth or falsity of a fact or proposition, including (a) facts and admissions of parties, which are properly called evidence; and (b) presumptions of either fact or of law, and citations of law. (2) The conviction, assurance, or certainty generated in the mind by the presentation of evidence and argument in support of a judicial proposition. (3) Documentary evidence, as affidavits, deeds, etc., offered in the trial of a cause. (5) The state or quality of having successfully undergone a proof or test. SYNoNYMs: Attestation, certification, confirmation, demonstration, essay, evidence, ordeal, test, testimony, trial."

And note the opposites or antonyms of "Proof":

"Assertion con'ecture dis roof failure fallacv I I Y J l' p)).) fancy, imagination, refutation."

From this, perhaps, we can gather the important negative fact that "AssERT1oN," at least, is not salesmanship.

THE GENERAL sERvIcE DEPARTMENT AMERICAN WRITING PAPER COMPANY JOSEPH A. BORDEN, DIRECTOR

lo SOUTH LA SALLE STREET, CHICAGO, ILL.

PUBLISHERS

AMERICAN WRITING PAPER COMPANY

JOSEPH A. BORDEN, DIRECTOR

Io SOUTH LA sALLE STREET, CHICAGO, ILL.

PuELisIiER's

Many other things are important, but correct definition is indispensable... go from definition to definition. Run down the meaning to its last retreat.... In thousands of instances words run like railroad trains on the same track till they come to the fine points of a switch, where the usage of the language sends them off in diflerent directions.... By intelligent study of the dictionary you will soon learn how one definition opens up the way to another. Thus a subject may be traced through the dictionary and something added at every point to fulness and meaning.... In the quotation the definition comes to vivid life. The quotations sustain, as they often inspire, the definitions. —Introductor_y to Funk 53 Wagnalls New Standard Dictionary.

It is an impudent kind of sorcery to attempt to blind us with smoke (A _ssERT1oN) without convincing us that the fire has existed.

— funius.

Assertion, unsupported by fact, is nugatory; surmise and general abuse, in however elegant language, ought not to pass for proofs.

—— funiur

A COURSE IN WRITING PRINTED SALESMANSHIP 5-9 A COURSE IN SELLING PRINTED SALESMANSHIP

EGINNING with the term "show" we have followed a series of authoritative definitions without break in relation or sequence, testing our structure as we proceeded and finding each unit to be solid and rigid and sound down to the term "mind" — to find that to be "a collective term for all forms of conscious intelligence." And thus we came to bedrock. And thus we know that the structure we are building stands on a foundation that is firm and stable and true.

To change the simile we have traversed a highway and at all forks have taken the direction which definition sign-posts have indicated, and, as a consequence, we find ourselves on a smooth and substantial roadbed of thought and fact.

But suppose we take a cautious run down one of those fair-looking forks, just to see Where it leads and what happens to others we constantly see traversing it? All right. Let's go!

rs NToNYMs," says the Standard, "have the I E advantage of definition by contrast. The meaning of a word is often made clearer by the sharp statement of what it is not; as when we note that pure signifies 'Not adulterated or mixed'; 'Not defiled, polluted, sullied or tainted'; 'Not immodest or indelicate. ' "

The meaning of a situation or condition is also made clearer by the sharp. statement of what it is not and I think this will hold in the contrast of mere "Advertising" as against AdvertisingSelling, or PRINTED SALESMANSHIP.

If we follow definitions faithfully, in relation and sequence, we must eventually see if we are right or wrong, for assuredly we shall be brought up against conditions that will very emphatically tell us so.

Here is a fork; the sign tells us to keep to the right, but we will branch to the left and discover whence this road leads and to what it leads and then determine if we wish to continue on it.

"BOASTING. Proud and vainglorious speech; bragging; self-assertion'."

Now comes:

"BRAG. I; To declare or assert boastfully. To deceive or overawe by boasting; bluff; 2. To speak of oneself or one's own afifairs in a boastful, vainglorious manner; vaunt oneself; to swagger; strut; show off. The act of bragging; boastful, bragging or arrogant language."

"BRAGGADOCIO. 1. Pretentious brag or boasting; empty vaunting; swagger. 2. One who talks boastfully; a swaggerer."

Now to:

"BLUFF. (I) Bold or boastful speech or manner intended to intimidate or deceive with regard to one's real strength and resources."

Now to:

"VAINGLORIOUS. Filled with vainglory; vain
to excess of one's own achievements or attainments; as, a vainglorious person; VAINGLGRY: To engage in idle boasting. Excessive, pretentious and demonstrative vanity; glory, pride or boastfulness that is vain or without grounds; undue elation or self-congratulation."

Now to:

"VAUNT. (I) To speak of boastfully; brag of or about; as, to vaunt one's deeds; (2) To display with ostentation; exhibit proudly; as, to vaunt one's grandeur in public.

" 'The vaunting of new linens and woolens. ' — George Eliot, "Romola."

"I. To make a boastful AssERTIoN or ostentatious display of one's own worth, attainments, achievements or the like; boast; brag. VAUNTER. One who vaunts; a boaster; braggart."

And now to:

"VAIN. I. Proud of petty things or of trifling attainments; elated with self-admiration, as of one's person, dress, deeds, possessions or attainments, and craving admiration from others; greedy of applause. 2. Showing shallow fiippancy; giddy; silly; as, a vain trifler. 3. Ostentatious, showy; said of things; as, vain trappings. 4. Unproductive of useful or satisfying results; ineffectual; worthless; fruitless; useless; unprofitable; as, a vain search. 5. Without any substantial foundation; empty; unreal; void; as, how vain is human praise. French and Latin; vanus, empty.

"Synonyms: Abortive, baseless, bootless, deceitful,-delusive, empty, fruitless, futile, idle, inconstant, ineffectual, profitless, shadowy, trifling, trivial, unavailing, unimportant, unreal, unsatisfying, unsubstantial, useless, vapid, worthless."

And that's the end of that road.

"Compare," says the Standard:

"Effective, efficient, firm, potent, powerful, real, solid, sound, substantial, valid, valuable, worthy."

Ay, compare them indeed! In the comparison you have the true and the false; will you take your clients over the road of AssERT1oN, Boast, and Unsupported Claim till the morass of failure engulfs, or will you keep to the solid road of Demonstrative, Educative, and Alfirmative copy that leads to success?

BY this time it will perhaps be apparent that there are two great types of "copy" or "presentation" that we might broadly designate as (I) Supported; (2) Unsupported. In parallel columns we might get an approximate classification as below: '

SUPPORTED CoPY UNSUPPORTED Co1Y Affirmative copy Assertive copy Evidential copy Boasting copy Demonstrative copy Blufl-ing copy Believable copy Bragging copy Reasoned copy Shallow-silly copy Logical copy Puffing copy Educational copy Vaunting copy Explanatory copy Giddy-fiippant copy Informative copy Vainglorious copy Convincible copy Claiming copy Transparent copy Opaque copy

The terms overlap, but that can hardly be avoided. Two terms introduced, i. e., "Transparent" and "Opaque," will be further dealt with as we proceed. A further term introduced, i. e., "Evidential," may be defined now:

"EVIDENTIAL. Of the nature of, or 'furnishing evidence. "

It manifestly relates to "evident" and the definition of that term will probably help us materially in an ultimate process of condensation:

"EVIDENT. Plain or manifest, as to the mind or to the senses; clearly perceptible; obvious; indubitable; as, evident facts; his success was evident; serving as evidence; conclusive.

"Synonyms: Apparent, clear, conspicuous, discernible, manifest, obvious, palpable, patent, perceptible, plain, tangible, unmistakable, visible.

"EVIDENTLY. In a manner to be perceived or understood; obviously;' clearly; in a manner to convince the mind; manifestly; certainly."

It will be seen that the term "Evidential" relates to evidence and proof in a legal sense, to clearness in a literary sense, and to conviction in a logical sense, hence I believe we can divide (' 1, ' '

Copy Into four main types: (3) AsSERTIvE CoPY (4) OPAQUE CoPY (1) AFFIRMATIVE CoPY (2)Ev1DENT1AL CoPY

IT would be as well to get distinctive differences in mind'at this stage. Suppose we find an advertisement like this:

No. 1.

That, manifestly, is an unsupported assertion, claim or statement. You can run down your

"Unsupported Copy" column and class it by any term you find there that you deem fits it.

You may consider the announcement a boast, a bluff, or a brag, and the very essence of all these is lack of support, as that couplet of Longfellow's indicates:

"Big words do not smite like war-clubs,

Boastful breath is not a bow-string."

— Hiawatha.

The credulous reader may accept the statement; the skeptical reader may not. The bigger the claim, the greater the number who, automatically, will reject it; the stronger assertive copy is, the greater is the multitude repelled by it.

But supposing the advertisement reads this way:

That would be an AFFIRMATIVE advertisement. You will remember the com arin illustration

' ' (I)7 p g given in assert:

"Almost any criminal will assert his innocence; the honest man will seldom lack means to vindicate his integrity."

We might paraphrase this as follows:

"Many advertisers assert that they have the best, but the man who has the best will seldom lack the data necessary to show it."

In the case of the second advertisement the booklet,of course,would be the instrument through which the Hartmann Company would prove its case.

The reason you should catch this distinction between AFFIRMATIVE and EVIDENTIAI. and AssERTIVE advertising is because one is practically forced to the AFFIRMATIVE or AsSERTIvE type in using periodicals where every line costs tremendously (as in The Saturday Evening Post, for example, with its page rate, per issue, of $7,000).

In such a publication you would not look for EVIDENTIAL copy, because to show, adequately and conclusively, that the HARTMANN PIANo was the best piano made would require, by the very nature of the case, a great deal of space (perhaps sixteen to twenty-four pages) and that would cost (computing on the sixteen page basis) $1 I 2,000 per issue, or over $6,000,000 per annum, for one publication alone. "

NDER space charges such as above, one makes a U statement and conjoins it with proof, this proof being made available by the mere act of asking for it. The reader of announcement No. I (pure assertion) may reject it at once as "boast," "bunk," "brag," "lying," or what not, but if he read announcement No. 2 he could hardly dismiss it in that summary way because, apparently, he would be doing violence to truth if he did and he therefore accepts the statement tentatively or reserves judgment till he has had an opportunity to peruse the booklet.

It will be seen that the mere linking of a booklet (or other medium) with an announcement such as is cited gives it SuPPoRT and establishes a BRIDGE over which the skeptical can reach the advertiser and over which the advertiser can reach the skeptical. The AFFIRMATIVE advertisement appeals on rational and reasonable grounds for a full hearing, and frequently gets it —much more frequently than does the AssERTIVE advertisement which is dealt with there and then and, ofttimes, none too gently.

Later we shall see that there is the AFFIRMATIVE and AssERTIvE letter, and that the principles we expound in periodical work apply with equal force in Direct-Mail work. At present it will sufiice if you remember that:

AssERTIvE copy makes UNsuPPoRTED statements or claims.

AFFIRMATIVE copy makes SUPPGRTED statements or claims.

AssERT1oN ignores the need of evidence.

AFFIRMATION recognizes that need.

AssERTIoN goes into the box without witnesses.

AFI-'IRMATION has its witnesses in the court room.

ASSERTION may state truth — but

AI-'FIRMATION says, Here is the proof of my statement if you need it.

There is a tremendous difference between the tactics of Assertion and Aflirmation, as may possibly be glimpsed even at this stage; that difference will be accentuated as these Lessons proceed.

E now have "Evidential" copy to consider. It could, of course, be in periodical advertising if the thing advertised could have its claims proved easily and quickly in relatively small space, or in comparatively large space (one or two pages for instance), but, ordinarily, we do not expect to find it in periodical space. The correct place for "Evidential" copy is in the booklet with which the business answers inquiries. AsSERT1vE or AFFIRMATIVE copy should NOT be in the booklet. The booklet is the court of last resort, as it were, and from its data the buying verdict will be drawn, hence it should be evidential in the highest degree. The "woof" or "weft" of material is:

"The cross-threads in a web of cloth. "

The "warp" of material is:

"The threads that run the long way of the fabric."

So EVIDENTIAL copy should be a related and cohesive web of words; long threads of reason, demonstration and explanation should criss-cross it till the reader sees a believable and convincible pattern in the fabric of words.

The copy loom will work true and fair with right materials. The How of THAT will come when this preliminary education in materials has passed. To make bricks we must use the materials of which they are composed; we want, not alone form and shape, but substance. So are made good bricks, and so is made sound copy— copy that sells — — PRINTED SALESMANSHIP.

THE GENERAL sERvIcE DEPARTMENT AMERICAN WRITING PAPER COMPANY JOSEPH A. BORDEN, DIRECTOR
IO SOUTH LA SALLE STREET, CHICAGO, ILL.
PUBLISHERS

When you doubt, abstain. —Zoroaster.

Doubt comes in at the window when inquiry is denied at the door.— Prof. Yowett.

The first requisite of style, not only in rhetoric, but in all compositions, is perspicuity. — W hately.

Obscurity in writing is commonly an argument of darkness in the mind. The greatest learning is to be seen in the greatest plainness. —— Wilkins.

When you doubt between words, use the plainest, the commonest, the most idiomatic. Eschew fine words as you would rouge, love simple ones as you would native roses on your cheek. —— Hare.

There is a certain majesty in plainness. — South.

Something further is necessary to that lively interaction of mind and object which we call a state of attention; and this is interest.

-A COURSE IN WRITING PRINTED SALESMANSHIP 6-9 A COURSE IN SELLING PRINTED
SALESMANSHIP

ET us go back for a moment to the two columns of "Supported" and "Unsupported" copy in Lesson No. 8. If you will carefully compare the qualities of the contrasting classifications given therein, you will realize that "Supported" copy tends to create conviction (because it is verified or verifiable), while "Unsupported" copy tends to create doubt or suspicion (because it lacks the elements of verification or substantiation).

You get the psychological or mind effect in these two contrasting definitions:

" DOUBT. " CONVICTION.

"The state of suspended "The state of being conjudgment through lack vinced;firm belief founded ofcertain knowledge. on evidence; the act of Uncertainty as to fact; producing mental conINDECISION in belief or viction;.. . forcing acopinion... an OB-knowledgment of the EcTIoN. SYN.: disbelief, truth. 'Lincoln trained distrust, hesitancy, in-himself to be the foremost credulity; misgiving; convincerofhis day.'" question; skepticism; suspicion; unbelief."

URTHER on, please carefully note, we condensed F the different classifications of "Supported" and "Unsupported" copy into four terms, comprising: (I)AssERT1vE CoPY. (I) AFFIRMATIVE CoPY. (1) OPAQUE CoPY. (2) EVIDENTIAL CoPY.

Kindly recollect that these four terms contain Within them the twenty-two classifications of copy given in the "Supported" and the"Unsupported" columns of Lesson No. 8.

This is done because four terms are easier to recollect and handle than twenty-two; nevertheless you should know what is behind those terms because you may be very frequently asked to explain what you mean when you term "copy" AssERT1vE or OPAQUE, or AFFIRMATIVE or EvIDENTIAL.

I think the nature of AFFIRMATIVE copy Was pretty thoroughly explained, but we might pause a little more on EVIDENTIAL copy. Mr. W. Stanley Jevons, in his Science Primer of "LooIc," says: The STANDARD defines logic as: "The science or doctrine of correct thinking; the principles governing the reasoning faculties in the pursuit and exposition of truth." A working knowledge of logic is therefore most useful to the man wishing to write EviDENTiAi. copy, and, for a working outline of that science in simple, understandable form, I can think of no better work than "LOGIC" by W. S. Jevons. It is sold in New York, Cincinnati, and Chicago by the American Book Company and costs less than one dollar. I would advise a perusal of this work, not necessarily to study and master the science, so much as to get a working idea of it; for general purposes an intelligent understanding of the broader principles of logic will be quite sufiicient.

"Perhaps the most common cause of bad reasoning is the use of AMEIGuous terms, which mean one thing in one place and another thing elsewhere. A WoRD WITI-I Two DISTINCT MEANINGs Is REALLY TWO
WoRDs."

Now "Evidential" has a number of different meanings, as we saw in Lesson No. 8, "Relating to evidence and proof in a legal sense, to elearness in a literary sense, and to conviction in a logical sense," and I want you to be sure to catch that fact because some men in attempting to show that my principles were not always applicable have stated that my method or idea always is to prove a thing. I think it ought to be clear that it is nothing of the kind. Proof is one of the factors to use in writing business copy, when it is required, and as it is required, but I think it is clear by the "Supported" copy column of Lesson No. 8 that one may be required to TEAGH, EXPLAIN, REAsoN WITH, or INFORM; as a matter of fact, conditions may be such that "copy" has not to be carried to the last degree of proof or demonstration, and still fall within the classification of "EVIDENTIAL" copy (in one light, at least) if it is BELIEVABLE.

In other words, "EVIDENTIAL" copy may mean absolute or relative proof, absolute or relative teaching, absolute or relative explanation, absolute or relative reasoning, or absolute or relative information, the degrees between ABsoLUTE and RELATIVE being tempered by the nature of the case and the circumstances surrounding the thing or service being advertised. This means that "Snow" must be pushed to the buying point. Where that is, judgment must say. _

If you remember that copy in general must be cast in the general mold of "Snow" you will have grasped the general principle involved. Your Judgment as to ways and degrees of SHOWING will develop as you work.

Because "Evidential" copy has a number of meanings I have placed the term opposite "OPAQUE," because, while "EVIDENT," as we saw in Lesson No. 8, means, "Plain or manifest, as to the mind or senses," "OPAQUE" means, in its literal sense, "Impervious to light; not transparent or translucent," and in its figurative sense: -"Unintelligible; obscure; as, an opaque style." -So you see:

BAD COPY is: GOOD COPY is:
AssERTivE._ ' AFFIRMATIVE.
OPAQUE. EvIDENTIAL.

Please get these four terms and their meanings firmly in mind, because you will want to use them constantly in preparing copy, judging copy, criticising copy, or reviewing copy, either in the form of periodical or mail advertising; that is, you will have to be constantly asking yourself:

"Is this AssERTIvE or OPAQIJE?" or: "Is this AFFIRMATIVE or EVIDENTIALP"

You will find that these four terms will cover the characteristics of a very large proportion of copy (probably 90 per cent of all copy). There are exceptions that fall outside, just as the English language has irregular verbs, etc., but we will take up these exceptions in detail later and try to make them easily recognizable when met.

The only term that will be likely to cause you trouble is "EVIDENTIAL," but it will not if you remember that in trend and effect it tends toward:

A clear, logical, reasoned, educational, or informative way of treating a presentation or subject. ' '

HILE on this point it may be the proper place to discuss another. Some students seem to think that I am trying to teach them a method of WRITING different from that they already possess. This is hardly correct. If you possess the faculty of expressing yourself clearly and accurately I would hardly wish to change your STYLE at all. You can let it stay right where it is, and use it in the perfect confidence that it will be all right. What I want you to do is not to WRITE differently, but to collect your DATA differently. This will perhaps be clearer ifI illustrate this way: Situated six miles from where this is written is one of the famous flying stations of the United States Government. Supposing you are an author and I am an editor and I said, "Go out there and get a story for Saturday's paper," you would in all probability assume from such generalized instructions that I wanted a story of "human interest" and you would go out and interview-the various airmen and record various thrilling experiences, which in due course you would shape up into an article of absorbing interest to a great number of readers.

But suppose after reading your article I said: "Charlie, I guess it's my fault, but Iwas rushed at the time and didn't give you sufficiently definite ideas as to what I wanted. This is a splendid article, but it doesn't cover the points I need. I want you to go out again and give me an article showing how ejjfciently the United States Government handles or manages its air stations." You would then approach the flying station in a different attitude, and collect very different data from what you gathered at first. To do this you wouldn't have to change your writing style, but you would simply apply it to a different subject. Your style and individuality would remain a fixed factor—— your subject alone would have changed.

Now, if your style is simple and clear, keep it; do not think I want to interfere with it. I simply want you to apply that method and style to facts got for AFFIRMATIVE or EVIDENTIAL treatment, rather than to facts got for AssERTIvE or OPAQUE treatment. I want you to keep your INDIVIDUALITY and simply to approach PRESENTATION with a different end and object and aim in view that will tinge your whole attitude, cause you to seek the right class and type of facts and information, which, when under your hand, you can present in your own clear and characteristic style.

Of course, if your style is not clear, there will be something to learn and adopt; but if it is, keep to it. I say this because some students in the past, under the impression that they had to WRITE DIFFERENTLY, became stilted and self-conscious in their EXPRESSION METHODS. That is a bad fault to develop simply because my ideas are misconstrued. If, on the other hand, you find your STYLE is not good, then it would be as well gradually to perfect it; but don't worry too much about your STYLE——it's your ATTITUDE toward a proposition that counts. You are not to come at it as a literary man seeking a reputation through rhetorical eflects, but as a barrister or lawyer seeking a verdict on EVIDENCE.

If you can put plain statements in plain words,

' you are equipped to go far, once you get the right viewpoint or attitude in which you are to approach a business with the ultimate idea of presenting it, through PRINTED SALESMANSHIP, to the public.

NDER "Supported" copy column (Lesson No. 8) U I think we have grouped the main elements of copy with one exceedingly important exception; the remaining element is INTEREsT. An illustration of the meaning of that term is given by the STANDARD as follows:

"3. PEDAGOGY. The effort of attention on the part of the pupil encouraged by the endeavor of the teacher to make his subject attractive."

By defining the last term I think we will sufficiently appreciate what "Interest" means:

"ATTRACTIVE. Having the power or quality of" attracting; drawing forth sympathy, affection, or interest; as, an attractive style. SYN.: agreeable, alluring, engaging, enticing, fascinating, interesting, inviting, pleasant, pleasing, tempting, winning. ANT.: abhorrent, deterrent, detestable, disagreeable, forbidding, repellent, repugnant."

Different ways of arousing and sustaining INTEREsT will be treated as we proceed; at present it is sufficient to remember that our system or plan most emphatically and decidedly embraces INTEREST. I emphasize that point here because opponents will urge that a system based on reason is cold and hard and repellent to the general public; that, to a certain extent at least, is quite' true,—but our system does not rest in pure reason but only on it as a base or foundation, as it were, that, like all foundations, is very frequently out of sight with the copy structure bathed in an atmosphere of glowing interest.

One of our tenets is-to Snow attractively.

This not alone holds as regards psychical presentation (via words and ideas), but also as regards physical presentation (through format, design, dependent art, etc.).

We take everything in the world that can be utilized to help to sell, in its right proportion and time and place.

Things that do not help to sell, however useful or beautiful they may be in other places, have no use for us.

The good salesman, in addition to being a good teacher, a good logician and reasoner, is also a mighty interesting man, and a man that we find, as a rule, is exceedingly well dressed because he appreciates the value of appearance in selling. We should be all that he is, and not less than he is, and it should be clearly understood that we are.

Let no competitor therefore class you as an apostle of ugliness simply because you discard beautiful things that have no selling service, or as an advocate of pure, cold reason simply because reasons and facts constitute the base or foundation of your structure.

The oral salesman and the writer-salesman have much in common. The writer-salesman, as his brother salesman, can be tactful, diplomatic, persuasive; he can be forceful, masterful, and authoritative; he can be pleasant, friendly, and sincere; he can be a good logician or a good teacher, a good demonstrator or a good informant; he can work on the brain or on the emotions; he can plead, suggest, or request——he can do any or all the things that circumstances point out as necessary or advisable to do to make sales at a profit. All . that limit him are the boundaries of BusINEss, and they in all truth are wide enough, far-flung enough, for any conceivable thing that business may attempt to do, or that he may attempt to do for business.

N examining our "SUPPORTED CoPY" column (Lesson No. 8) we find factors of Evidence, Demonstration, Reason, Logic, Education, Explanation, Information, etc., and these are both perceived and visioned best when bathed in the light of PERSPICUITY, meaning:

"Clearness of expression or style; the logical method of conveying an author's meaning unmistakably; free. dom from obscurity, intricacy, or ambiguity; lucidity

"'We are commonly taught that pcrspicuity depends upon a proper choice of words, a proper structure of sentences, and a proper order in the whole composition;... but it supposes distinctness in our conceptions.' — Thomas Reid.

"SYN._: clearness, distinctness, explicitness, intelligibility, lucidity, plainness, translucency, transparency.

"ANT.: Ambiguity, cloudiness, confusion, incomprehensibility, indistinctness, intricacy, obscurity, unintelligibility, vagueness."

We have recently had a little talk on style, etc., during which I said, "If you can put plain statements in plain words, you are equipped to go far." If you can do that, as a matter of fact you have a gift. Value it and keep to it and realize that great truth which H. W. Shaw uttered when he said:

"Successful writers learn at last what they should. learn at first — to be intelligently simple."

AMERICAN WRITING PAPER COMPANY
JosEPii A. BORDEN, DiREcTOR
IO SOUTH LA sALLE sTREET, CHICAGO, ILL.
PUBLISHERS

The best style of writing, as well as the most forcible, is the plainest. — Horace Greeley.

The safest words are always those which bring us most directly to facts. — Chas. H. Parkhurst.

In the world there is nothing great but man; in man there is nothing great but mind. —— Sir W. Hamilton.

Read not to contradict and confute, nor to believe and take for granted, nor to find talk and discourse; but to weigh and consider. — Bacon.

Reason is mistress and queen of all things. — Cicero.

A COURSE IN WRITING PRINTED SALESMANSHIP E9' A COURSE IN SELLING PRINTED SALESMANSHIP

E will recollect that Lesson No. I I ended with Lincoln's statement that he was never satisfied till he had taken a thing that was dark or obscure to him and studied it out till he could put it: "In language plain enough... for any boy I knew to comprehend."

Lincoln afterwards "sold" verdicts to juries in a most efficient way—he showed such juries Where truth and justice lay.

He afterwards just as efiectively sold himself and his policies to the American people through his power of clear, lucid statement.

This matter of clarity, clearness, perspicuity, is of exceedingly great importance in PRINTED SALESMANSHIP, and, in showing, one should leave no stone unturned to show clearly. In other words, do not confound the act of showing with actual showing. Your intent to show may be there; nevertheless you may not really show, or you may show ohscurely. In such event you have failed.

To realize how tremendously important clearness and plainness are in PRESENTATION, let us go back to our column of SUPPORTED CoPY (Lesson

No. 8), convert the terms we find there into nouns, and then briefly define them again. We will then see that the sumpof the definitions is making plain, thus:

EVIDENCE..........That which makes evident.

DEMONSTRATION.....A pointing out.

REASON...........That which explains.

LOGIC.............Exposition—interpretation of meaning.

EDUCATION.........Instructi0n — teaching — teach making known or understood.

EXPLANATION.......Elucidation, making plain, understood, or intelligible.

INFORMATION.......Kn0wledge... practical understanding.

IN Lesson No. 5 it was asked:

"Now what is salesmanship? We have in prior Lessons seen the form or shape through which it works (Attention — Interest — Desire — Action), but that, metaphorically speaking, is only the shape or form of the brick and not the substance of the brick itself, and as we must know the Jufistance of bricks before we can manufacture them, so also we must know the substance of salesmanship before we can achieve it."

We then set about finding and gathering our substances, tailing them as we found them by authoritative definitions and finding they conformed to all stress and strain requirements.

We finally assembled those substances under "Supported Copy" (Lesson No. 8), and later coalesced them into two parts or terms, i.e.,

AFFIRMATIVE CoPY.

EVIDENTIAL CoPY.

E have talked a great deal about trans

PP parency, clearness, plainness, elucidation, and the like, and I think we are thoroughly im pressed with the great IMPORTANCE of those factors.

It is important to understand that they are all embraced in the term "Evidential."

We have talked a great deal about logic, reason, proof, etc., and it is important to understand that they are embraced in the term "Evidential."

We have talked of the value of evidence and testimony, and it is important to understand that they are embraced in the term "Evidential."

It is important to understand, in short, that "EVIDENTIAL," as used in these Lessons, is an embracing or generic term, mothering the family of evidence, demonstration, reason, logic, education, explanation, information, clearness, etc.

I would like this to be perfectly clear because these terms, being of one great family, relate and interrelate and lap and overlap.

In the future, then, when I talk of EVIDENTIAL copy you will know I am using a GENERIC or MGTHER term for clearness, logic, reason, proof, testimony, etc., and, on the other hand, when I talk of clearness, perspicuity, logic, reason, proof, evidence, etc., you will know they are children of the mother term being partieularized and discussed in the relation implied by the text. Sometimes it is necessary for me to emphasize the necessity for proof or evidence or testimony in some classes or types of copy; opponents in the past have jumped to the conclusion that I insisted on proof in all types of copy. This is manifestly

» wrong; some copy is best written in a teachable or informative vein, other copy in an explanatory vein, etc., therefore I have sought for a term and an angle that would embrace them ALL—the angle is to SHOW (not necessarily to prove), and the term is EVIDENTIAL, which covers showing, proving, teaching, etc.

Further, please recognize that the formula for SAi.EsMANsHIP (which we adopt) embraces INTEREsT, i.e., Attention — INTEREsT — Desire —— ActiOn, and this frees us from the charge of favoring presentation based on cold, repelling reason alone.

We can, if necessary, reduce our elements or ideas to three fundamentals: (I) To SHOW.

(2) To SHOW evidentially. (3) To SHOW evidentially and interestingly or ATTRAcTivELY.

The terms embraced under "SUPPORTED COPY" (Lesson No. 8), while they all have different meanings, still have related meanings. They are in a very logical sense synonyms of each other. Begin with one term and progressively trace the terms it yields and you will inevitably come to the other terms.

Note how Lincoln, the great reasoner and debater, instinctively used the words "Plain language" in the second last paragraph of his answer in Lesson No. II. Note how Mr. McBain (same Lesson) instinctively used the words "Proof," "Reasoning," "Demonstration," "Evidence," "Logical," "Convincing," in talking of factors that made a good SALEsMAN.

Do you not see that selling is showing?

When you realize that there are degrees in showing, just as there are degrees in a barometer or a thermometer, and that it is the degree of showing injected that marks the degree of salesmanship attained, then you are on the high road to results.

The showing can be: (I) Good.

(2) Bad.

(3) Indifferent.

ust as the thermometer can be at:

(1) 70 Summer heat.

(2) o Zero.

(3) 32 Freezing point.

As it approaches Summer heat crops begin to grow, flowers begin to blossom, fruit begins to mature. The analogy holds in salesmanship. As you approach "Good," results will come, and they will come better and more quickly as you approach: (I) Good.

(2) Better.

(3) Best.

In "SUPPORTED CoPY" (to change our similes) we find our tools. We must now learn how to use them.

In other words, I think this is as far as it is necessary to carry this demonstration of AFFIRMATIVE-EVIDENIAL copy. Hereafter I will take it for granted that you take it for granted and I will consider this foundational premise finished, tested, and accepted.

This, therefore, concludes the first and most important section of our Course.

HE following is taken from Lesson XIII of T"LEssoNs IN LOGIC" (W. Stanley Jevons, M.A., author; The MacMillan Company, New York, Publishers) and mirrors the method I have endeavored to follow in preceding Lessons of this Course:

"It may be doubted says Mr. Jevonsl whether any man ever possessed a more acute and perfect intellect than that of Blaise Pascal. He was born in I623, at Clermont in Auvergne, and from his earliest years displayed signs of a remarkable character. His father attempted at first to prevent his studying geometry, but such was Pascal's genius and love of this science, that, by the age of twelve, he had found out many of the propositions of Euclid's first book without the aid of any person or treatise. It is difficult to say whether he is most admired for his mathematical discoveries, his invention of the first calculating machine, his won derful Provincial Letters,... or for his profound Pensees, or Thoughts, a collection of his reflections on scientific and religious topics.

"Among these Thoughts is to be found a remarkable fragment upon Logical Method, the substance of which is also given in the Port Royal Logic. It forms the second article of the Pensees, and is entitled Reflexions sur la Geometrie en general. As I know no composition in which perfection of truth and clearness of expression are more nearly attained, I propose to give in this lesson a free translation of the more important parts of this fragment, appending to it rules of method from the Port Royal Logic and from Descartes' celebrated Essay on Method. The words of Pascal are nearly as follows:

" PASCAL ON METHOD

"The true method, which would furnish demonstrations of the highest excellence, if it were possible to employ the method fully, consists in observing two principal rules. The first rule is not to employ any term of which we have not clearly explained the meaning; the second rule is never to put forward any proposition which we cannot demonstrate by truths already known; that is to say, in a word, to define all the terms, ' and to prove all the propositions. But in order that I may observe the rules of the method which I am explaining, it is necessary that declare what is to be understood by definition.

"'We recognize in Geometry only those definitions which logicians call Nominal Definitions, that is to say, only those definitions which impose a name upon things clearly designated in terms perfectly known; and I speak only of those definitions.

"'Their value and use are to clear and abbreviate discourse by expressing in the single name which we impose what could not be otherwise expressed but in several words; provided nevertheless that the name imposed remain divested of any other meaning which it might possess, so as to bear that alone for which we intend it to stand.

"'For example, if we need to distinguish among numbers those which are divisible into two equal parts, from those which are not so divisible, in order to avoid the frequent repetition of this distinction, we give a name to it in this manner:—-we call every number divisible into two equal parts an Even Numaer.

"This is a geometrical definition, because after having clearly designated a thing, namely any number divisible into two equal parts, we give it a name divested of every other meaning, which it might have, in order to bestow upon it the meaning designated.

"Hence it appears that definitions are very free, and that they can never be subject to contradiction, for there is nothing more allowable than to give any name we wish to a thing which we have clearly pointed out. It is only necessary to take care that we do not abuse this liberty of imposing names, by giving the same name to two different things. Even this would be allowable, provided that we did not confuse the results, and extend them from one to the other. But if we fall into this vice, we have a very sure and infallible remedy;— it is to substitute mentally the definition in place of the thing defined, and to hold ' the definition always so present in the mind, that every time we speak, for instance, of an even number, we may understand precisely that it is a number divisible into two equal parts, and so that these two things should be so combined and inseparable in thought, that as often as one is expressed in discourse, the mind may direct itself immediately to the other.

"'For geometers and all who proceed methodically only impose names upon things in order to abbreviate discourse, and not to lessen or change the ideas of the things concerning which they discourse. They pretend that the mind always supplies the entire definition of the brief terms which they employ simply to avoid the confusion produced by a multitude of words.

"Nothing prevents more promptly and effectively the insidious fallacies of the sophists than this method, which we should always employ, and which alone suffices to banish all sorts of difliculties and equivocations.

"'These things being well understood, I return to my explanation of the true method, whichconsists, as I said, in defining everything and proving everything.

"'Certainly this method would be an excellent one, were it not absolutely impossible. It is evident that the first terms we wished to define would require previous terms to serve for their explanation, and similarly the first propositions we wished to prove would presuppose other propositions preceding them in our knowledge; and thus it is clear that we should never arrive at the first terms or first propositions.

" 'Accordingly in pushing our researches further and further, we arrive necessarily at primitive words which we cannot define, and at principles so clear, that we cannot find any principles more clear to prove them by. Thus it appears that men are naturally and inevitably incapable of treating any science whatever in a perfect method; but it does not thence follow that we ought to abandon every kind of method.... The most perfect method available to men consists not in defining everything, nor in defining nothing and demonstrating nothing, but in pursuing the middle course of not defining things which are clear and understood by all persons, but of defining all Others; and of not proving truths known to all persons, but of proving all Others. From this method they equally err who undertake to define and prove everything, and they who neglect to do it in things which are not self-evident.'

"Pascal's views on the geometrical method," continues Mr. Jevons, "were clearly summed up in the following rules, inserted by him in the Port Royal Logic.

"'(I) To admit no terms in the least obscure or equivocal without defining them.

"'(2) To employ in the definitions only terms perfectly known or already explained.

"'(3) To demand as axioms only truths perfectly evident.

"'(4) To prove all propositions which are at all obscure, by employing in their proof only the definitions which have preceded, or the axioms which have been accorded, or the propositions which have been already demonstrated, or the construction of the thing itself which is in dispute, when there may be any operation to perform.

"'(5) Never to abuse the equivocation of terms by failing to substitute for them, mentally, the definitions which restrict and explain them.'

"If says Mr. Jevonsl we steadily bear in mind, in studying each science, the necessity of defining every term as far as possible, and proving each prop. osition which can be proved by a simpler One, we shall do much to clear away error and confusion.

"I also wish to give here the rules proposed by the celebrated Descartes for guiding the reason in the attainment of truth. They are as follows:

"'(I) Never to accept anything as true which we do not clearly know to be so; that is to say, carefully to avoid haste or prejudice, and to comprise nothing more in our judgments than what presents itself so clearly and distinctly to the mind that we cannot have any room to doubt it.

"'(2) To divide each difliculty we examine into as many parts as possible, or as may be required for resolving it.

"' (3) To conduct our thoughts in an orderly manner, commencing with the most simple and easily known objects, in order to ascend by degrees to the knowledge of the most complex.

"'(4) To make in every case enumerations so complete, and reviews so wide, that we may be sure of omitting nothing.'"

THE GENERAL SERVICE DEPARTMENT AMERICAN WRITING PAPER COMPANY JOSEPH A. BORDEN, DIRECTOR
I0 SOUTH LA SALLE STREET, CHICAGO, ILL.
PUBLISHERS

A COURSE IN WRITING PRINTED SALESMANSHIP 8-' A COURSE IN SELLING PRINTED SALESMANSHIP

AMERICAN WRITING PAPER COMPANY
JOSEPH A. noRnEN, DIRECTOR
Io SOUTH LA sALLE s'rREET, CHICAGO, ILL.
PUBLISHERS

"Reasoning or Discourse, then, may be defined as the progress of the mind from one or more given propositions to a proposition different from those given. Those propositions from which we argue are called Premises, and that which is drawn from them is called the Conclusion. The latter is said to follow, to be concluded, inferred or collected from them; and the premises are so called because they are put forward or at the beginning (Latin prae, before, and mitto, I send or put). The essence of the process consists in gathering the truth that is contained in the premises when joined together, and carrying it with us into the conclusion, where it is embodied in a new proposition or assertion. We extract out of the premises all the information which is useful for the purpose in view— and this is the whole which reasoning accomplishes."

— jevons, "Lessons in Logic."

A COURSE IN WRITING PRINTED SALESMANSHIP 5-" A COURSE IN SELLING PRINTED SALESMANSHIP

F selling is, in essence, showing, we must learn what to show and how to show. In doing this digressions may be necessary, but, at the end, it will be seen that these all bear a very clear and definite relation to the main theme which is to S H O W.

If you will give some study to "copy" in which you sense the sales urge or buying urge, you will find, as a great rule, that it embodies these principles of formation or construction: (I) It passes the reader through four stages or zones comprising ATTENTION-INTEREST-DESIREACTIoN.
(2) There are three phases to the message, i. e., INTRoDUCTIoN-PREsENTATIoN-CoNCLUsIoN. (3) It progresses usually from AEsTRACT to CoNCRETE or in other words from GENERAL))) to SPECIFIC. ' (4) It lays down initial PRE1vIIsEs which run to VERIFICATION in final CoNcLUsIoNs.

In Lesson No. 4 the REAsoN for casting a sales message in ATTENTIoN-INTEREsT-DEsIRE and AcTIoN form was indicated and illustrated.

In Lesson No. 3 we saw a number of "Sign' advertisements — that is, advertisements without relling force.

On page 9, however, we found one with selling force — the Postum advertisement.

With the aid of illustrations given in Lesson No. 4 you will be able to trace the steps of Attention-Interest-Desire-Action in this Postum advertisement.

You will note the "Introduction" in these words:

"Many people get the idea that they can keep their nerves on edge and their digestion upset year after year and 'get away with it.' They sleep only half as much as they should— and never get properly and thoroughly rested."

The above is, of course, abstract and general. The writer comes to the more specific "You" in the following paragraphs, though he is still in the "Introductory" stage:

"If you tire out easily, if you are getting pale and anemic, if your food does n't digest as it should, would it not be well to stop and consider whether coffee or tea is having its effect on you?

"The caffeine and theine found in coffee and tea are drugs, as any doctor can tell you. Is it any wonder that the steady use of these drugs sometimes causes serious damage?"

Note that to above point the writer (who is selling PosTUM) has said nothing whatsoever about the thing he has to sell—he is in the realms of the "abstract" or "general." Note now, however, he begins to close in, beginning PREsENTATIoN (talk about the thing he has to sell) in the last line of the following paragraph:

"If you really want to be fair with yourself, and give yourself the opportunity you deserve in order to do your best work, make up your mind to quit coffee or tea for a while — and drink delicious, appetizing Postum instead."

And continues:

"Postum permits sound, refreshing sleep which builds strength, energy, and endurance.

"Order Postum from your grocer today. Drink this hot, refreshing beverage in place of tea or coffee for ten days and see what a wonderful difference it will make in the way you feel."

The writer of this advertisement, it will be seen, began in a kind of "General Interest" zone, i. e., about "Many people" and the "nerves of many people" and "Nature" and passed on to a specific or concrete thing called "Postum" and "You" which he eventually relates to "people who tire easily" and are "pale and anemic" and who do not "sleep half as much as they should" and who suffer from indigestion, etc.

You see that a bond of common interest is struck before an attempt is made to sell Postum.

The writer premises that Postum will bring sound, refreshing sleep and other natural boons to those suffering from insomnia caused (inferentially) by undue indulgence in coffee, tea, etc.

His method of demonstration is through a pack age of Postum and his assumption is that such a package can be bought at such a low price that no one suffering as indicated will hesitate to test the truth or otherwise of the statement made, through such a purchase.

This method answers fairly well on a very lowpriced commodity.

If the commodity is high-priced, however, people will not buy to test. They will only buy when they are sure.

A man may buy a package of Postum to test its worth, but he will not buy a piano to test its worth.

In buying a piano its worth has to be pretty well shown to him before he makes the purchase.

Hence, a piano advertisement cast in such a strain would not be so successful as a Postum advertisement.

In some respects, then, the Postum advertisement complies with selling requirements:

It has ATTENTION-INTEREsT-DEsIRE-AcTIoN zones.

It has INTRODUCTION-PREsENTATIoN-CoNcLUSION.

It progresses from AEsTRAcT to CONORETE.

It lays down PREMIsEs which run to VERIFIcATIoN.

It is not affirmative in the sense that it offers no booklet. It is not evidential because it does not prove its case or contention in its presentation. It offers to prove in its product, relying on low price to cause purchase that it hopes will cause demonstration by physical test in lieu of conviction through evidence or reasoning.

In many analogous cases advertisers proffer a free sample, and that, undoubtedly, strengthens the appeal.

EFORE examining other "copy" it might be as well to define several terms that have occurred in the Postum case and be sure about their meaning, etc. The STANDARD is our authority, as usual.

"PREMISE. 1. To say or write as an INTRODUCTORY statement, as in ExPI.ANATIoN; as, to premise some particulars. 2. To propound as the premise or basis of argument.

'In the beginning of a treatise, it is proper and necessary sometimes to premise some praecognita or general principles.' — WATT.

"To lay down as an antecedent PROPOSITION, provision, or condition; stipulate; assume. Premit."

"PREMISE. A proposition laid down, proved, supposed, or assumed, that serves as a ground for argument or for a conclusion; a judgment leading to another judgment as a conclusion.

'The truths known by intuition are the original premises from which all others are inferred.' — MILL, Logic."

We will now pass on to:

"PROPOSITION. 3. Rhetorical. That which is proposed as a subject of discourse; the part of a discourse in which the subject is enunciated; in a poem,

I use advertisements as examples for the reason that, being compact, they admit of easy reproduction. While they illustrate principles in highly skelezonized form, that is suflicient for explanatory purposes.

the part setting forth the theme. 4.. Math. The statement of a truth to be demonstrated."

Premise and proposition, it will be seen, are practically synonymous. The mathematical definition, "The STATEMENT of a truth to be DEMONSTRATED," will, it may be seen, fit the Postum case. Later, we will see, a great deal of advertising is in the form of a mathematical proposition, i. e., "The statement of a truth to be demonstrated," and we will see that while AFFIRMATIVE advertising (by proffer of a booklet or other media) leads to such demonstration, AssERTIVE advertising (offering no book or other media, nor evidence in the advertisement itself) does not demonstrate its truth or its supposed truth.

We will now get the definition of CoNc1.UsIoN, and we ought to note carefully that it has two meanings, one being:

"The act or process of finishing or ending a thing," conclusions in this sense being in all advertisements, letters, etc., and, of course, In the Postum advertisement; the other meaning Is:

"4. A thing believed in consequence of investigation or reasoning; any matter of inferential conviction; as, the conclusion of the jury was that the man was innocent. 5. Logic. A proposition the truth of which is inferred from a premise or premises; especiallythe third proposition of an Aristotelian syllogism; as, the conclusion that the Indians have rights follows from the premises that the Indians are men and that men have rights....8. Rhet. THE CLos1NG PART or A DIscUssIoN oR DIsCoURsE, OFTEN INCLUDING A RECAPITULATION, PRACTICAL APPLICATIGN or THE ARGuMENTs AND STATE1vIENTs ALREADY CoNsIDERED,AND A PERoRATIoN.

'Some remarks on this topic may form a not unsuitable conclusion to the present article.' — CIIANNING.

"Law. 3. A finding; as a conclusion of law or fact. Conclusion of fact, a conclusion as to the existence of a given fact, drawn from testimony."

It will be noted that the Postum advertisement may comply with definition No. 4, "Asthing believed in consequence of investigation," provided the investigation is made by the purchase of a package, but that the announcement would not comply with the logical definition (No. 5); that the rhetorical definition is lacking from the announcement altogether, and that it does not comply with the legal definition inasmuch as it does not prove its case by testimony.

Conclusions in all these senses are almost invariably found lacking in current advertisements, in letters, in folders, and in most booklets.

I n other words, advertisers are stating truths but not proving them.

Others, of course (it is to be hoped they are greatly in the minority, though that is an open question), are not stating truths and (for very obvious reasons) are as a consequence not even attempting to prove them.

In other words, some bad advertisers are poor logicians by intent, while some good advertisers are poor logicians by ignorance or default.

The public, looking on, exercising its subcon

These brief excerpts from definitions will serve to make clear the fact that we can best lead into or up to a highly particular or special subject by beginning in thoughts or ideas common to all, or "to a large number or proportion," because, while the special subject of itself and by itself (as Postum) may have no interest for the large majority which a common experience (such as health, for instance) will have, so we seek to link up "generals" to "particulars" and show a relationship which affects the reader or auditor (as in Postum).

The Einstein Theory of Relativity may not interest you of itself, but I may eventually interest you in it if I show its relationship to something that does interest you (astronomy, for instance). A boy may not be interested in geometry of itself, but if he wants to be a sailor and I lead him to that science through navigation he will be apt to become interested in it.

We may go from HEALTH to PosTuM. " " Nemo Corsets. " " Physical Culture Magazine. " " McGovern's Gymnasium. " Madison Square Garden Swimming Pool. " Dr. Lust's Sanitarium. " Grape Nuts. " " Sporting Goods of Aber crombie 55? Fitch, etc.

In such cases an easy and natural transition is from the general subject of health to the special subject of Postum, Corsets, Physical Culture, Madison Square Garden Swimming Pool, etc., or, in other words, from the GENERAL to the SPECIFIC.

You have an interest in the general subject and you are educated to an interest 'in the specific subject as the PREsENTATIoN unfolds.

To repeat: good "copy" progresses usually from ABsTRACT to CONCRETE, or, in other words, from GENERAL to SPECIFIC.

The above is the order or sequence as it unfolds to the reader. The copywriter, however, is behind the scenes and his method, prior to drawing the curtain, may be different. _

AEsTRACT to CONCRETE works from out in—it works from a mass of things to a single thing.

There is the reverse step of course, i. e., working from the concrete to the abstract — from the special to the general — from a single thing to a mass of things.

This is beautifully illustrated in that wonderful lecture to working men by Huxley on "A Piece of Chalk" wherein, "Beginning with a piece of crayon, which he held in his hand, he led his readers, without a break of interest and with the introduction of hardly one outlandish word, from the most familiar experiences of everyday life out into the furthest reaches, the most sublime generalizations of geology and cosmogony. " This, in logic, is simply the inductive and deductive processes of reasoning: deduction draws from a mass of facts in the observation of a single thing; induction works from a single thing back to the mass of laws or phenomena that governs it.

It will be perceived that such a method would not "Sell" the piece of crayon, because the reader's mind was being led away from it.

If Huxley had been a manufacturer of crayons, however, with the same gift of expression he would (in the privacy of his advertising library or studio) have worked back from the piece of chalk (a specific thing) to a point where he was among things of general human interest (as in the midst of his splendid lecture), drawn his advertixing curtain at that point, appeared before his audience and taken them back over the ground he had traversed, to that piece of chalk.

You see this in the Postum announcement, skeletonized though it is; the writer worked from Postum to Nature before he crystallized his message; the message works from Nature to Postum, however.

There are limiting zones with this method, of course. Huxley spent the entire time allotted to the lecture in taking the audience back to those magnificent generalizations whence sprung creation itself. If he were selling a specific product like crayons he would not want to go back to such distant boundaries, but with a few deft strokes would start somewhere near his subject (as nearly as he could get in terms of common or usual interest) and as deftly "link up."

The Postum announcement is not held up as a model of perfection but it illustrates the process. It comprises in all 258 words. "Postum" is not mentioned till the I 59th word. The division here is I59 words for INTRODUCTION, and 99 words for PRESENTATION (a conclusion in the rhetorical sense is lacking).

INTRODUCTION may seem to have a disproportionate part of the announcement, but this is not really so; we will see that at times INTRODUCTION may be very long; at times it may be quite short. To illustrate: a number of years ago I wrote a prospectus for a life insurance company; it ran to probably twenty thousand words; practically nineteen thousand of these were "INTRooUcT1oN," the PRESENTATION and CoNcLUsIoN being summed up on two pages, but behind the last thousand Words were the weight and momentum of nineteen thousand. In other words, the mind of the reader was prepared for a certain definite and irresistible CoN-cLUsIoN as the "copy" progressed, and (to make a paradox) the endwas reached before it was reached. In other words, the reader had sold himself before I attempted to sell him, so that final PRESENTATION and SUMMING UP (CoNcLus1oN) merely confirmed his resolution to buy.

In this particular case I found my elements of interest in the suhject itself, and that, of course, is always a fine thing to be able to find. It is always a thing it is very advisable to look for... no use wandering round the North or South poles, or taking the reader there, if all you want is in the city where you are.

AMERICAN WRITING PAPER COMPANY
JosEPH A. BORDEN, DIREcToR
IO SOUTH LA sALLE sTREE'r, CH1-CAco, ILL.
PUBLISHERS

"Monsieur Iourdain, an amusing person in one of Moliére's plays, expressed much surprise on learning that he had been talking prose for more than forty years without knowing it. Ninety-nine people out of a hundred might be equally surprised to hear that they had long been converting propositions, syllogizing, falling into paralogisms, framing hypotheses, and making classifications with genera and species.

"... All people are logicians in some manner or degree, but unfortunately many people are bad ones, and suffer harm in consequence.... The weakest framework with the most logical mind will conquer in the end, because it is able to foresee the future, calculate the results of actions, and to avoid mistakes which might be fatal.

"Reason is the mind's eye... and the logician endeavors to learn exactly what this reason is which makes the

A COURSE IN WRITING PRINTED SALESMANSHIP 69 A COURSE IN SELLING PRINTED SALESMANSHIP

REVIEWING Lesson No. I 3 it should be pointed out that at No. 2 I used the word "Presentation" in a sense slightly different from its prior use. This will continue through these Lessons,

" hence it might be as well to have both senses under stood. I regard PRE-sENTAT1oN in one sense as the whole of the copy (as the copy of ax booklet), and in another sense as part of the whole; the difierence, as in most words with two or more meanings, will usually reveal itself from the sense of the text. In speaking of a booklet, for instance, I might say "The Presentation as a whole is not good," in the sense defined by the Standard:

"The manner of bringing into view or thought; way of putting; exhibition; representation; also that which is represented; as, his presentation of the case."

The second sense in which I use PRESENTATION 1S to separate it from and contrast It against INTRoDuc-TIoN and CONCLUSION, thus:

INTRODUCTION
PRESENTATION
CONCLUSION.

This order, or sequence, in a booklet comprising what is in reality three chapters or three definite sections, the first (Introductory) beginning (usually) in an abstract or generalized form, leading into the second (Presentation), which is an intensely specific and concrete representation of the goods or services offered, and the third (Conclusion) being a Reeapitulation or the PERORATION (as in a long speech).

We will deal more definitely with this CONCLUSION, RECAPITULATION, or PERORATION as we proceed, and it will be sufficient to point out here that a Conclusion in the Recapitulation sense is seldom found in periodical advertising. The reason for this is quite obvious, as Recapitulation is only called for on a prolonged literary or oratorical effort, and periodical advertisements are of necessity brief, hence do not require final review or summing up.

It might be as well to define those terms here for the sake of clearness:

"RECAPITULATE. I. To repeat again the PRINCIPAL points of; go over again in CoNc1sE review or SUMMARY; sum up, as an argument. II. To repeat concisely what has already been stated at length; give again in order the principal points, heads, or topics."

"RECAPITULATION. 2. Rhetoric. A form of peroration in which the respective processes, as of explanation, conviction, excitation, and persuasion, pursued in a discourse, are CONCISELY repeated for the purpose of more complete effect."

"PERORATION. The CoNcLUs1oN of an oration; especially a concluding part in which the speaker makes practical application of the subject to the audience.

It may be explanatory, confirmatory, excitatory, or persuasive, or may take the general form of recapitulation.

'As the champion of New England closed the memorable peroration of his reply to Hayne the silence of death rested upon the crowded Senate chamber.'

— MA'rHEws, Oratory and Orators.
"

A prolonged, intricate, or statistical PREsENTATION (as in a booklet) making big and as a consequence DIFFICULT sales requires a CoNCLUsIoN that may partake of the nature of RECAPITULATIoN, CoNCLusIoN, or PERoRATIoN in such degree as the particular circumstances call for.

One of the great defects of many commercial booklets is that they are all PREsENTAT1oN. Introduction is either very crude or non-existent. Conclusion — there is none at all.

Because of this the ordinary booklet is really only one-third of a booklet — '— it is two-thirds incomplete by every standard through which orators and writers reach results.

IN our review of the PosTUM announcement we saw that:

"It was not aflirmative in the sense that it offered no booklet, and it was not evidential because it did not prove its case or contention in its presentation. It oflered to prove by its product, relying on low price to cause purchase that it hoped will cause demonstration by physical test in lieu of conviction through evidence or reasoning."

In other words, the POSTUM announcement left a GAP; like a broken footbridge it was narrow enough for a reader to jump if he wanted to, but if he did not want to he might turn back; in other words, by refusing a free sample (for demonstrating purposes) or, in lieu of that, by failure to proffer a booklet, POsTuM raised certain Obstacles to a complete getting together.

The NUJOL advertisement herewith reproduced shows a better way. The PREsENTATIoN may cause a reader to buy and reach conviction through demonstration (always best if it can be done), but the coupon at the bottom takes care of those who refuse to buy, though they may still be open to conviction, by offering A BOOKLET, and this makes the announcement AFFIRMATIVE, and, I think, in that relation at least, its superiority to the PosTUM announcement will be evident.

As a matter of fact, advertising should base on and spring from a booklet, or, in other words, the booklet should be the foundation of the advertising.

Personally, when approaching an advertising campaign I insist on writing the booklet first. I base periodical advertising on the booklet. The booklet as a consequence automatically becomes a logical part of the advertising.

The BOOKLET is in fact the crystallizing, coalescing, dovetailing and binding-together element of the campaign — the fusing, blending, uniting element — the brief upon which the presentation is from preventable disease. Yezoelasd perts in the extension of life that physical breakdown, disease, evennld age and death, areall either preventah e or postponable.

But to prevent or postpone them you must avoid constipation and resulting toxemia‘. "To no other single cause," writes a distinguished physician, “is it possible to attribute one-tenth as many various and widely diverse disorders."

Take diabetes for example. An eminent specialist whose observa tion has covered thousands of cases, states: "Constipation is nearly always found present in persons suffering from this malady. It will always be found that constipation existed before the appearance of sugar. The writer has no doubt that chronic constipation is one of the‘ most prolific causes of the rapid increase of diabetesinall civilizedcomsnussities. The statistics gathered by the United States Census Bureau show a death rate nearly tentimes as great as twenty years ago.” A se rious condition in itself. But truly alarming when ou realize that over ‘ three-fourths o all disease can be traced directly or indirectly to eonstipation.

built, and a business advertising without a booklet is a business revealing an inherent defect. We might pause on this Nujol. announcement long enough to see that it parallels the PosTUM announcement in many respects; we can trace the respective steps of ATTENTION-INTEREST-DESIREAcTIoN clearly through it. It has an INTRODUCTION and PRESENTATION (with, of course, a formal conclusion or ending). It progresses from ABSTRACT to CONCRETE (the “You” in headline undoubtedly being used in the general or abstract sense in which one would address an audience) and it lays down initial PR1-:M1sI-:s which run to VERIFICATION in final conclusion.

Analyzed, we find the main announcement (dealing with NUJOL) runs to 423 words; NUoI. is not mentioned till the 318th word, consequently 318 words are devoted to INTRooUcTIoN, and I06 to PRESENTATION and CoNcI.usIoN. Here Introduction takes practically two-thirds of the whole allotment of words.

We have seen the copy is AFFIRMATIVE, therefore we can hardly expect it to be EVIDENTIAL, though it would have been stronger if the “distinguished physician” had been mentioned by name, and page or folios of U. S. Census Bureau data cited for reference, and the “eminent authority” also named.

The presumption, however, is that these citations will be found in the EVIDENTIAL booklet. "Leading hospitals throughout the world" will also be cited, no doubt.

IN connection with both the PosTUM and NUJOL announcements the rhetorical definition of “ PERsUAs1oN ” will be in order outlined as follows:

“(5) Rhet. The department of invention in which the object is to move the will, in order to lead to a new choice or course of conduct. It embraces (1) PERsUASION PROPER, in which motives are presented to lead the hearer to the direct formation of a positive purpose, and (2) DISSUASION, in which the object is to change some dominant purpose.

‘ In persuasion, the object of discourse is to move the will, either by leading it to a new act or purpose, or by dissuading it from one already adopted/”

We see the principle of DIssUAs1ON employed in the POSTUM announcement:

“Make up your mind to quit coffee and tea for awhile.”

And in the Nujoi. announcement:

“Not by the use of laxatives or cathartics, for, Writes an eminent authority, ‘an inestimable amount of injury is done by the use of these intestinal irritants, most of which provide temporary relief only at the expense of permanent injury. ’”

The touch of a practiced hand is seen in the above in quoting an independent third party, freeing the NUoL people from any charge of bias on a matter that touches their sales closely, and, as stated, the name of the eminent specialist would have lent the final touch of skill and cleverness to the whole paragraph.

The Po1NT to be carefully noted in both cases is that PosTUM is a BEVERAGE (like coffee and tea) and it becomes very important to show an UNSELLING point of distinction in relation to coffee and tea. NUo1. is taken for constipation (like laxatives and cathartics) and it becomes of equal importance to UNSELL the public on those laxatives and cathartics in order to give NUoL an unopposed field.

In writing announcements, therefore (periodical advertisements, booklets, letters, etc., being all embraced),remember the principle of DISSUASION and apply it dexterously and effectively as needed. In the case of NUJOL a mere attack on constipation would not accomplish much, as there are a thousand and one remedies on the market designed to alleviate that condition, but when those are shown to be "Dangerous and injurious" they are_ summarily swept aside in favor of NUoL.

Finally note how each advertisement:

"Shows an advantage through positive moving words that demonstrate the advisability of seizing it... a gain that it is an incentive to take."

MONEY, earnings, profits, have a universal call to men, and in that generalized subject the .National Salesmen's Training Association seeks its Introductory Approach. Here the respective and orderly zones of AT'rENT1oN-INTER-EsT-DEs1RE and AcT1oN are clearly perceivable, from the

Ii

I

And lhne is. In lhe G111 pllzq they dhmveml I "Ill _11._1 11.1.1.1 1....1.... .. T111. n1..1....1111.11 in. 11 111.110 1. 1.. 11.. s.1.1. 11.1..1 1........... s.1... ......1. 11......v 1.1. 1.11..4.1...y......-1.... 11.....1.1..1.1. 11...........1.1 1.1.11. 1.1. 1.. T1». 1.... 11...11. 1.,...1..1.1. 11.. 1. 1.11.1. 1.1.1 1.....1 11..11....._11... 11. 1. 1...111.1...1-1.. N. 1.11.11 11.11 1.. .. 1111 1.-1. s.1.........1..." 11. 1.111..... PU.

A...11..11.1.¢.11.....1..11..'s _ 11.1.1. 1...1s.i111..11.1....-11... 1. 111.111. 1.. 1.11.1 1.. mi. 1.1.11.1 so....1 11».......... .i.....1 1.5.1.... 1.1.1.11. 111.111.1111 1.1 1;. 1.... 11...» 1111.... 1...1..1..1...-1. 11.a 111.114.1111.1111.. . 1111. 111-. 1...1..1 11.. 11. 1.111.... 1. 111.111 111n1b.=11 11......" TM.1..11 1114-s.1.A 11.1 1...:

Have Done It!

New Way to Enter Thin Field individuals who, heading the announcement, literally SPEAK proof, through the headline, down through the body to "Master Salesmen" secrets, to the final ACTION-WORKING COUPON, which also makes the advertisement strongly AFFIRMATIVE in character and effect. '

The National Salesmen's Training Association is mentioned in the fourth from last paragraph, consequently about two-thirds of space and type is employed for INTRoDUcTIoN.

It will be noted that this advertisement meets the requirements of a sales document: (I) It passes from Attention to Action.

(2) It has Introduction and Presentation (also formal conclusion). (3) It progresses from abstract to concrete (the "You" in headline being used in the same sense as one might address an audience). (4) It lays down initial premises which run to verification in final conclusion.

In one sense it ranks higher than the NUJOL announcement inasmuch as in addition to being AFFIRMATIVE it is also EVIDENTIAL (names and addresses being cited) and in photographic reproductions of successful students it embodies principles ofVERisIMILITUDE.1'

A distinction between this and the NUJOL and POSTUM announcements should be carefully noted, the National Salesmen's announcement not seeking to sell outright, but merely seeking to get or " Sell" an INQUIRY.

1'VERisiMiLITUDE will be touched on later in these manuals.

It also:

"S/zows an advantage through positive moving words that demonstrate the advisability of seizing it... a gain that it is an incentive to take." '

Probably this is as far as it is necessary to go in this direction, as we have examined three advertisements that, on examination, seem to have the selling urge, and we have dissected them one by one to find where it was and how it operated.

We began with a good advertisement, went to a better, and finally ended in a BEST with reasons for growing superiority clearly shown.

It should of course be understood that with these examples, and with all others that are given throughout, we are concerned merely with excellence of technical construction and form, and have nothing to say as to the merits or otherwise of the concerns themselves.

AMERICAN WRITING PAPER COMPANY

JOSEPH A. BORDEN, nmscron

IO SOUTH LA SALLE STREET, CHICAGO, ILL. '

PUBLISHERS

FOREWORD

Sound selling advertisements are tabloid prerentationx. They lend themselves readily to reproduction, whereas it would be physically diflicult to reproduce booklets, etc., on an extensive scale.

Constantly keep in mind that principles drawn out of periodical advertisements reproduced in these Lessons are directly applicable to letters, folders, booklets, and other MAIL MEDIA.

Later, letters, and sections of booklets, etc., will also be reproduced.

PRINCIPLES of SELLING COPY, however, are applicable to all copy, whether in the form of periodical copy or booklet or letter copy— it is important to keep that point in mind.

When PRINCIPLES are mastered, ALL Kmos of advertising-selling will be mastered with them.

A COURSE IN WRITING PRINTED SALESMANSHIP 6-9 A COURSE IN SELLING PRINTED SALESMANSHIP '

IN order to get a view of our subject as many sided as possible we will now consider a number of advertising announcements of varying characteristics. As we proceed we shall endeavor, so far as we can, to indicate the type or class into which each announcement falls.

The advertisement of the EssEx MoToRs is EVIDENTIAL in character. The absence of boast or claim on the part of the Company is noticeable. There is praise in the announcement, but it comes, as it should, from third parties.

A buyer instinctively and intuitively assumes that bias exists when a man is selling his own goods or his own services, and, as a buyer, is constantly watching for manifestations of this bias. He heavily discounts claims.

Testimony (from third parties) stops this discounting to a very great extent. Facts stop it. Proof stops it. In periodical or booklet "copy," always keep this psychological fact in mind:

Proof is not a Statement of truth, but

Evidence of the truth of the statement.

"'Evidencc' is and must be the test of truth, and is, I suppose, the ultimate ground on which we believe anything. — M1vAR'r, Nature and Thought. "Evidence includes the testimony of witnesses." — Standard Dictionary.

"A person of undoubted veracity may state (through ignorance or misinformation) what is not the truth."

" 'To be veracious, it is only necessary that a man give utterance to his convictions; to be true, it is needful that his convictions have afiinity with fact.'"

— Standard Dictionary.

This advertisement originally appeared in The Saturday Evening Post, a periodical with a great general circulation, as almost every one knows. In reaching "the general public" it is usually wise, as we have seen, to preface the product or services being sold with an Introduction. There is practically no Introduction in this announcement, its sponsors no doubt relying for ATTENT1oN and INTEREST on the almost universal interest in automobiles. In other words, they have calculated, doubtless, that interest was in the suhject itself. Under such conditions one hardly need abstract openings, but can get right into the subject ——-this should be carefully noted.

The advertisement would be infinitely better if it offered a BOOKLET to extend its story.

A subsequent variation of this advertisement that would strengthen and improve it would be the photographic reproduction of the various publications that endorsed the ESSEX car. We see this idea illustrated in THE PRINTING ART announcements immediately following the EssEx cOpy.

A printed testimonial is much weaker than if photographed and reproduced in its original form

This is the principle of VERisIMILITuDE which the STANDARD defines as:

"The character or quality of being verisimilar.

(I)Resemblance of truth; probability; likelihood;

(2)Close adherence to truth or REALITY, as in A REPREsENTATIoN; REALisM."

In short, Evidence by reproduction of the original documents.

G.--I-r and shape, and where testimony or proof or evidence hinges on important documents one should always study how to reproduce them in the nearest approach to VERISIMILITUDE possible.

The WHITE TRUCK announcement differs from the Essex announcement inasmuch as it does n't cite testimony but gives an exhaustive list of well-known concerns from whom testimony can be procured.

We might term this announcement both EVIDENTIAL and AFFIRMATIVE, inasmuch as means of verification' and investigation are automatically placed at the disposal of the skeptical in such form that there is apt to be very little skepticism about it.

INTRoDUcT1oN is practically absent, it being assumed, as in the EssEx announcement, that the subject itself has sufficient general interest.

The very prominent display of headlines and of "WHITE TRUcxs" "links up" at a glance, as it were. The advertisement in one sense is a verbal P1cTURE, its IMPORT and IMPLICATIONS being caught in a few seconds of time without the necessity of minute study or close perusal of word after word. If the headline is read, "WHITE TRUcIs" embraced, and close-clustered body details apprehended As A WHoLE, a tremendous INFERENCE is taken out of the announcement.

This advertisement, like the EssEx advertise lment, would be infinitely strengthened if it ofiered a hooklet.

A booklet made up of letters from the firms cited, reproduced by photography, would be an exceedingly convincing document; or photographed letters from leaders among those cited, with the letters of the lesser lights printed, would also be very effective, especially if, on this foundation of fact and proof and evidence, a selling presentation were reared.

It is very difiicult to understand why these great concerns ignore the tremendous potentialities for business that a booklet carries.

"DEMoNsTRAT1oN," says the STANDARD, is: "4. The exhibition and description of examples," and "DEIv-IoNsTRAToR" by the same authority is: "(2) A salesman who exhibits to customers the operation and possibilities of a machine or process." In that sense the HAMMOND TYPEWRITER advertisement is undoubtedly demonstrative in characteristics and effect, as will be noted by the different styles and characters of type used in headlines, and specimens in border. In this typestyle reproduction we also find another example of VERISIMILITUDE. The advertisement originally occupied a single column in The Saturday Evening Post. It evidently assumes a sufficient interest in typewriting machines to eliminate the need of an INTRODUCTION. This advertisement offers two booklets, it will be seen (or rather assumed, because the coupon is so worded that it could be assumed that one might receive a machine instead of a booklet).

JEvoNs, in "Loolc," tells how we may LOOK at a thing and construct a correct mental

MESSAGE out of it:

"It is not only in scientific matters that we use hypotheses in order to learn, by correspondence with facts, what has been happening. We are continuously arguing in this way in the commonest affairs, and the mind often goes through all the four steps of preliminary observation, hypothesis, deduction, and verification in a few seconds. For instance, in looking out of the window into the street of a town, I see that the pavement is wet, instead of being dry, as it was an hour before. In all probability I at once consider what can have happened to cause the change. I form several hypotheses: rain may have fallen; a water-cart may have passed down the street; the turncock may have opened the water-pipes in the neighborhood. With great rapidity I draw DEDUCTIONS from these hypotheses. A water-cart does not usually water the foot paths, but rain would wet the footpath on one side at" least. Glancing at the footpaths

I see, perhaps, that they are dry. Rain, then, is probably not the cause; to be more sure I glance at the sky, and I find it apparently clear of clouds; this agrees well with the hypothesis of a water-cart, and I should be finally convinced if I discovered that the wet portions of the street ran in broad parallel lines nearly coinciding with the road way, or only slightly overlapping the footway, in the manner in which water-carts usually do their work."

In other words, we may be shown something that sets our powers of deduction, assumption. or inference in motion and from it we may construct (especially in advertising) a message that no one has literally said or no one has literally written.

It may indeed be planned that we do construct just such a message, and planned further that it will, when constructed, be favorable to the advertiser; he will not praise himself, but he will cause us to praise him; he will not say that he probably makes the best goods on the market, but he will cause us to say it.

The WILLARD people, it will be noted, give a

BATTERIEs (a mere itemization of names).

The reader, looking at this and grasping its gen-

eral import in one sweeping glance, is apt to argue, or deduce, or infer something like this:

"The car manufacturers itemized have the reputation of making good cars.

"They are strong, reliable manufacturers with ample financial resources, and they have ample means for testing every item of apparatus that goes on their cars.

"They have gained reputation, standing, and prestige by good work, not poor work; they would not be likely to put a poor battery on their cars.

"Because they equip with the Willard battery they tactically endorse it as a well-made battery — probably one of the best, if not the best procurable.

"Other batteries may be all right; but it seems to me this must be, therefore why should I gamble? I will buy a Willard."

You see, words cast in an afiirmative or evidential mold generate not alone other words, but other messages. This is undoubtedly what Arthur Brisbane meant when he stated that one of the arts of writing was the art of writing a hundred words that would make the reader think a thousand.

Remember the principle of INFERENCE when writing " copy" and know the class or type of copy in which it lays and that generates it.

The WILLARD advertisement, it will be seen, lacks an INTRODUCTION, and also lacks a booklet. It certainly would be infinitely stronger if it proffered a booklet, not alone as a bridge to sales, but as a claw to prospective buyers.

AMERICAN WRITING PAPER COMPANY
JOSEPH A. BORDEN, DIRECTOR
IO sour!-1 LA SALLE STREET, cmcnco, 11.1..
PUBLISHERS

Remember, SELLING is SIIow1No.

If you will study "Copy" in which you sense the sales urge you will find that, as a great rule: (I) It passes the reader through four stages or zones, i.e. , A'I'I'ENTION-INTEREST-DESIRE-ACTION.

(2) It has an INTRODUCTORY APPROACH. (3) It progresses (usually) from ABSTRACT to CoNcRETE— from GENERAL to SPECIFIC. (4) It lays down initial PR1-:MIsEs which run to VERIFICATION in final CoNCLUSION. (5) It Snows an ADVANTAGE (by inference or otherwise) which it is an INcENT1vE to take or seize.

— Roéert Ruxton

A COURSE IN WRITING PRINTED SALESMANSHIP 63-9 A COURSE IN SELLING PRINTED SALESMANSHIP

EVIEWING the WHITE TRUCK and WILLARD BATTERY announcements (Lesson No. I5) and contrasting them with such announcements as the NATIONAL SALEsMEN's TRAINING AssociAT1oN, for instance, we see that the two former lack a certain element of ATTRACTIVENESS that we find in the latter.

Yet we cannot deny the strength that inheres in WHITE TRUCK and WILLARD advertising as reproduced. If we analyze the matter we will see that the ATTRACTIVE element in the NATIONAL SAI.EsMEN's TRAINING AssoCIATIoN (and kindred announcements) lies in part in INTRODUCTORY tactics, and in part in INTERESTING text.

In the WHITE TRUCK and WILLARD announcements there is no introduction and no text— simply a group offavts. We might compare such announcements to -rocky promontories that rise, bleak and forbid ding, out of the sea, and still draw us by their stern, elemental aspects. As a matter of fact, the WHITE and WILLARD announcements find their STRENGTH in the EVIDENTIAL ruggedness that enwraps them. Each presents a great mass of basic facts.

It would be well to note carefully how EVIDENTIAL copy, crude though it may be, elemental though it may be, IMPREssEs. It is solid, foundational, primary, and simple, like the great things of the _ earth —— the things that endure through the ages.

The nearer we get to great basic facts the nearer we get rock-ribbed and ironbound qualities that impress with their stability and constancy.

A verifiable fact is a rock and a group of verifiable facts is a mountain.

E have seen that some announcements, relying on their own primal strength, dispense with booklets (always a great error of omission), and we have seen that others, partly selling in their periodical announcements, lead the reader over an attractive verbal bridge into the BOOKLET, where the presentation, free from the trammels of expensive periodical space, can be unfolded at sufiicient length to do it justice and to give it the final sales strength required to get the money. ' There is another type of announcement that, in lieu of featuring (or partly featuring) the service or product for sale, wholly ignores that in the periodical advertisement and features a booklet alone, relying on the booklet itself being "sold" by the announcement, and the booklet when in the hands of the "prospect" in turn selling the product or service offered. Such an announcement may not mention that there is anything for sale at all. A type of such announcement 1s seen in that of the AUTHORS'

F to lliiters!

WONDERFUL-BOOK—r-cad about itl Tells how easily Stories and Plays are couceived. written. perfected, sold. How many who don't DREAM they can write, suddenly find it out. l-low the Scenario Kings and the

. Story Queens live and work. How bright men

. _ and women, without. any special experience,

3 learn to their own amazement that their simplat Ideas may furnish hrll-liantplotsfor Plays and Stories. How one's own Imagination may provide an endless gold-mine of Ideas that bring Happy Success and Handsome Cash

4 'Royalties. How new writers get their names

' "-into print. How to tell if you AREa writer.

I How to develop your "story fancy," weave -clever word-pictures and uuique,' thrilling, reaT'sti'c f;lo£s. rf1;l0w your friends ma be your worst iudzes. How to avoid discouragement and the pi alls oi Failure. How to will

This surprising hook is abralulely frzz. No charge No obligation. Your copyis wilting for you. Write f_or_ it. MI, Just address

IN the VICTROLA announcement we see the BOOK or BOOKLET idea aptly and intelligently utilized in furtherance of the sale of Victor Records, the angle of approach or introduction being through the reader's interest in music, or his wish to acquire interest in it or information or education about it.

Here, what is virtually a GIFT in one sense undoubtedly generates sales and profits — an advertising illustration of: "Cast thy bread upon the waters; for thou shalt find it after many days."

In the BALTIMORE & OHIO announcement there is a very decisive use of the booklet as an instrument through which to sell TRANSPORTATION. The angle of approach or introduction in this case is a blend of patriotism, history, and love of travel. PRESENTATION in this announcement is skeletonized, but is doubtless amplified to the point of selling BALTIMORE & OHIO transportation against competitive lines, in the booklet.

We see a similar use of the booklet as a selling instrument in the announcement of the U. S.

Shipping Board, the angle of approach in this case being analogous to that of the BALTIMORE & OHIO, i.e., the lure of Europe, historical sentiment, and a proflered service.

In both announcements, zones of ATTENTION

INTEREsT-DEsIRE and AcTIoN are clearly traceable; INTRoDUcTIoN and PREsENTAT1oN (with formal conclusion) is patently evident, progression from ABsTRAcT to CoNcRETE is easily perceivable, and they both endeavor to SHoW—an opportunity for education, relaxation, and recreation, toward which the CoUPoN and BOOKLET acts as a step or bridge.

Nthe HARTMAN FURNITURE & CARPET CoMI PANY announcement (originally produced in colors) we see a number of different principles exemplified: First, the advertisement is based on "The lot for a little" idea, a profuse spreading out of what can be acquired marking it; this carries a physical appeal to the senses through the illustration and represents art applied to good selling purpose.

There is a strong play on the " Dollar down and a dollar a week" idea, making it seemingly easy to buy.

A strong attempt at outright sale is made, and (in a large number of cases) made successfully, no doubt.

CoNF1DENcE is inspired by the small first charge ($1) made with manifest value received in exchange. The conditions manifestly operate to prevent trouble or dissatisfaction.

In case the SALE is missed the BARGAIN CATALoG is strongly featured on the left and follows out the "Much-for-a-little" idea; note the "suggestive use of:

"Bargain" (always dear to a woman's heart).

"Great free 368-page Catalog."

cc----n

Amazing bargains In furniture. " Free trial of everything." fa

This is an excellent sales announcement, the sales stimulus being multiplied by:

The use of color (always a reliable stimulus to purchase). The use of art (in a depicting sense).

Skepticism is disarmed by easy first payment, possession for trial and judgment and firm guarantee. Through just such principles did Sears, Roebuck 81 Co. (in its earlier stages) lay the foundation for the wonderful business it has today.

The zones of ATTENTION-INTEREST-DESIRE and AcTIoN are clearly perceivable in this advertisement. While INTRoDUcTIoN is lacking, SALES URoE is strong through the goods (pictorially) being laid before the buyer.

The conception of the announcement makes it intensely specific and brings it right to the SALEs and INQUIRY point in a page of space.

It is a demonstration in itself, and proffers demonstration (and consequent satisfaction) to those acting on it. 1

This is probably one of the best pieces of selling copy we have yet examined, and it would be difiicult to improve on it in the space allotted. Mail order experience shows in every line of it and there is n't a point missed.

It will of course be understood that an offer and announcement such as this could only be constructed and made by a special type of firm. Mere financing of such selling calls for funds and resources beyond the average advertiser.

And, you will note, the HARTMAN advertise ment "Shows a gain that it is an incentive to take." I

ELIVERY for examination prior to payment is D confidence-breeding, and, when practicable, is sound salesmanship practice. You see this type of announcement in the PELTON PUBLISHING CoMPANY advertisement:

headline has a strong attention-getting value which the caption beneath holds. In column to left skepticism is alis-armed by EVIDENTIAL citations, giving extracts from letters of people who have benefited by purchase. Citation of prominent purchasers reinforces a favorable first impression. Note the IMPRESSION which a hasty GLANCE reveals:

"Free proof that I can raise your pay. "

" Send no money "

Here a desirable thing is offered, shown under conditions where no money is spent prior to being shown, and that implication is drawn out of a brief glance at the headlines. Examination simply strengthens the first hasty impression.

Attention-Interest-Desire and Action zones are clearly perceivable in this announcement in logical order and sequence.

Introduction and Presentation stand out clearly.

Progression is from abstract to concrete, the "You" being clearly collective in its sense.

The advertisement lays down initial PREMISES which run to verification in final conclusion.

The announcement points to an advantage that, if true, 1t would certainly be advisable to seize.

RaiseY6ur Pay

No matter how much you are earning now I can show you how

I have even taken failures and shown them ch week 8100. $200 and in many eases even more.

E will wind up this lesson by reproducing a type of advertisement that SELLs (for cash) a booklet that in turn sells SOMETHING ELsE (also for cash). In other words, a small sale of an advertising-selling brochure is made in the periodical space and a larger sale of something else is made in the larger booklet space. Such an announcement is reproduced below:

THE GENERAL sERvIcE DEPARTMENT AMERICAN WRITING PAPER COMPANY

JOSEPH A. BORDEN, DIRECTOR

lo SOUTH LA SALLE STREET, CHICAGO, ILL.

PUBLISHERS '

A COURSE IN WRITING PRINTED SALESMANSHIP 6- A COURSE IN SELLING PRINTED SALESMANSHIP

Lesson M. 17

From DEPARTMENT or GENERAL SERvIcE

AMERICAN WRITING PAPER CO.

Jos. A. Borden, Director

IO SouTI-I LA SALLE STREET

CHICAGO

PRINTED SALESMANSHIP 5' A COURSE IN SELLING PRINTED SALESMANSHIP lVritten Sxclasively for U. T. Q/Y. Trinters

BY

ROBERT RUXTON

THE GENERAL SERVICE DEPARTMENT

AMERICAN WRITING PAPER COMPANY

JOSEPH A. BORDEN, DIRECTOR

IO SOUTH LA SALLE STREET, CHICAGO, ILL.

PUBLISHERS

Proof is not a statement of truth, but evidence of the truth of the statement;

"I had six honest serving men

(They taught me all I knew);

Their names are What and Why and When

And I-Iow and Where and Who."

—Kipling.

"Evidence is and must be the test of truth." —Mivart.

A COURSE IN WRITING PRINTED SALESMANSHIP £9' A COURSE IN SELLING PRINTED SALESMANSHIP

E will continue our review of characteristic Wadvertisements in terms of Lesson No. I6. The JELL-O announcement (originally reproduced in colors) is a type of presentation that finds its power in an appeal to the senses. Dainty desserts, in original colors, almost literally set down before one, rouse the appetite, and hence

Desire.

While it is difiicult for a mere man to analyze a woman's mind, still I should think an additional incentive in such an announcement would be the desire of the woman to exhibit her culinary skill by making and serving such attractive dishes.

In many respects the JELI.-O announcement is allied to that of the HARTMAN (Lesson No. I6).

Color is an exceedingly valuable salesforee under many conditions, and, expensive though it is, it should be used far more frequently than it is. It will be noted that presentations of this character are as a rule specific and sell in the space, and the reason for this is that actual representation of the goods makes the advertisement a demonstration in a very large sense.

It w_ill be noted that announcements of this type comply with the principle of VERISIMILITUDE.

N the type of I DEMONSTRATIVE and VERISIMILAR we must class the BRENLIN window shade announcement; that is, it partakes of those elements. It is also AFFIRMATIVE in the fact that it offers a booklet. Itemization of factories and actual name and address of at least one prominent user— all tend to give the advertisement strength, and therefore to make it believable.

The text is illustrated (with samples for further physical demonstration)——a1l,itwill be noted, tend to SHOW idea or principle.

THE CONVERSE TIRE announcement is also de_ monstrative, it will be noted. Try the experi ment for yourself and see what it Snows you—see how it CoNv1NcEs you. The illustration' (large, ofmachine) is no doubt a concession to the artistic temperament of some director or ofiicer of the company, for I fail to see how it helps to sell tires. The text does, however.

THE HEEKIN COMPANY announcement gets its strength from its wide-flung and generous GUARANTEE. One feels that a firm that would guarantee its product under conditions that could easily lead to abuse must have profound faith in its product, and this faith conveys itself to the reader. He argues (by inference) that if the

Bake thing! I if isn't successfiil we'll fbr it ¢'I.r E know that any woman can gei'sueeesslul baking results with Heekin'e Pure Baking Powder For a better baking powder cannot be made. It is pure. It is strong. And Heekii-i's retains its strength until the last spoonful is used.

We are so confident that your baking will be successful with Heekin's, that we make what we believe to be the strongest guarantee ever oflered lor a baking powder!

Reed This Exceptional Guarantee

II ANYTI-Ilnu You BAx3—esi'ng fleekin'.r—d0es' not run Out to your el- llill selislaclion. llle price of the lull mi el baking powdel and an flrilte cl zl the illlredienu in Whatever you bah will be returned I0 you.

There are we "iI's," "ands" or "buts" lhflll this Iuillntee. Ii the on". biscuit: or uoy other loads you bake Ire not perleetly saeilllelery jun list the ingredients, their prises and the prise oi the biking powder. Send this lint to The Heekin coiuouuy. Cincinnati, Ohio, end your' money will be um you by mum mail.

You win agree that on'y die finest baking powder made could uiroui to be guaranteed no strongly Buy u can ioaiy- in use i._y_ou'n in-Heekiifl.

IHE HEEKIN coivii=A'NY, cuuouii, oiao

Heekin Company can afi'ord to take a chance like that he surely can afford to take the chance necessary to a purchase. He (or she) buys probably without any thought of falling back on the guarantee. It is n't arefund confidence that is inspired, but a confidence in the quality of the product.

HE wEsTERN COIL AND coMPANY's announcement has a difierent "MoTIi-"'; it takes (in semblance, at least) a judicial stand. It abstracts the conclusion of the investigation, leaves you to guess at it, and

ELECTRIC hence arouses both your curiosity and instinct for verification (you want to be shown). Verisimilitude is in this announcement in the repre

Something i; You Should " KNOW

Before you invest in any

Violet Ray outfit—you should know what high Irequency electric currents can and cannot do for the human e body. You oertainly want to know whether they are beneficial or harmful — ' whether you are making an ' _experim- cnt or making use ' of a universally proclaimed method ol treating various 1- disorders.

Know the Truth, , Read what S. H. Monell, 1 M. D., says about it in his book "The Truth About High Frequency." He tells . you in language that anyone

" can understand just what High Frequency Electric

'3 Currents can and cannot do for you. He is an acknowledged authority on electric therapeutics who tells the _ whole truth about the 'iolet Ray.

SEND for THIS BOOK

Slip J aim. Illlfi an envelope and. enclose iii. pon below rm ll 1 unbiased, an oratiw statement one who know: what the iole: Ray can actually do.

w. Clfl refer you to dealuu who '11 d(l'0n!!r3le mu.

'l-Ray-O outfit.

,ra.:..'.mT.:.:.:r.I...7-TR.

Enclolod mi HII' Fleuurm:

Nnma. _..........................

-1 I0: (oi UTHQ Tlulh about v.

"Moving or II'1'1PlllI'Ig force, whether in a literal or a figurative sense. ... A

--n predominant idea. —S. D.

sentation of the booklet. The conclusion (when gained) rests on the report of a physician, hence should be reliable and authoritative.

In my opinion the advertisement is weakened, however, by final lines above the coupon: "We. can refer you to dealers who will demonstrate reliable Vi-Ray-O outfits, "as this destroys the "Motif" or "Theme" upon which the "pull" is, based. Take out those lines and change name of concern, and you have a strong new theme.

A principle embodied in this announcement will be treated more voluminously as these Lessons' proceed, so study it carefully.

N the LA SALLE ExTENsIoN UNIvERsITY anI nouncement we have the "Story" type of advertising-selling. As this style of presentation has come into great vogue of late it should be carefully noted that the term "Story" has very dififerent meanings, and this, no doubt, is the place to define the term in full, as follows:

"STORY. I. A narrative or recital of an event or series of events, whether in prose or in verse, whether real or fietitious, or such narratives or recitals collectively; especially, a short tale, novel, or narrative of historical incident, usually with a climax; history; as, the story of Livy; a true story; a prize story. 2. A body of facts of special significance, told or untold, relating to a

Started Life as a Clothes Brusher Director of two Great Banks at 39

"Any man can get ahead who wants to,".says C. C.

Mollenhauer, and in this story he tells the secret of his rise from $2.50 a Week to his present position

or thing; as, there is a story conhouse; a person with a story.

particular person nected with that 3. Anything reported or told; a statement, report, or rumor; often used derogatorily; as, according to his own story he was the hero; there is an evil story abroad. 4. . The plot or intrigue of a work of imagination, as a novel, epic, or play; as, read the Odyssey for the story. 5. (Newspaper slang). An article in or contribution to a newspaper, other than an editorial; especially, reporters' work. 6. (Colloq.) A lie; a euphemism used chiefly by or to children. 7. An anecdote; as, a funny story. 8. A painting, sculpture, embroidery, or other work of art, representing a scene from history, romance, or legend.

Syn.: Allegory, anecdote, incident, narrative, recital, record, relation, tale. TALE is nearly synonymous with story but is somewhat archaic; it is used for an imaginative, legendary, or fictitious recital, especially if of ancient date; as, a fairy tale; also for an idle or malicious report; as, do not tell tales'; "Where there is no tale-bearer, the strife ceaseth. "

You see a story can be a relation of fact or a relation of imagination. It can be truth or it can be fiction, and "Fiction" is "The act of feigning or imagining that which does not exist or is not true."

Under the guise of the "Business story" much of pure fiction has been run, I am afraid, and, I am further afraid, many of the characters embodied exist only in the fertile imagination of the "story teller." To such types the announcement of the LA SALLE EXTENSION UNIVERSITY is a welcome relief. Note how the veracity of the text is proved by citation of the two banks with which Mr. C. C. Mollenhauer is connected; note how the photograph of Mr. Mollenhauer himself brings realism into the relation. Here is a story that can be verified to the hilt from facts which the announcement puts before all readers, and it stands in marked contrast to many "stories" in business form which fail to give the names, addresses, or photographs of relator or his characters.

Verisimilitude, fact, proof, and specific citation are especially called for in the "Business story," and, if they are absent, the whole presentation comes under suspicion. Statements made may be true, but they do not appear to be, hence they are not alone doubted, but received with skepticism and distrust by the public.

The "story" form of advertising reads easily and interestingly and is suitable for such conditions as call for it when backed by such citation and evidence as, for instance, are given by the La Salle Extension University.

Otherwise—otherwise, and very emphatically otherwise.

A COURSE IN WRITING PRINTED SALESMANSHIP 63 A COURSE IN SELLING PRINTED SALESMANSHIP

DEPARTMENT or GENERAL SERvIcE AMERICAN WRITING PAPER CO. Jos. A. Borden, Director Io SOUTH LA SALLE STREET

CHICAGO

AMERICAN WRITING PAPER COMPANY

JOSEPH A. BORDEN, DIREcToR

Io soUTH LA sALLE sTREET, CHICAGO, ILL.

PUBLISHERS

"Aiming at brevity I became obscure. "

' —Horace.

"The only use of a full and rich vocabulary is to express thought. Whenever the style gets in the way of the thought, smash the style. The thought is that for which we write. Will an exquisite style best express it? Then attain that if you can. But if the exquisite style is not the clearest and fittest, or if you cannot attain it, then give us a style less exquisite, so that the thought be expressed. " —:'ames C. Fernald.

"The INTRODUCTION is for the sake of the audience,— to awaken interest in the topic, so as to enable the reader... to start fairly with you. That is what the books of rhetoric mean by 'conciliating' the audience. Not that it is ever to be assumed that an audience is hostile, but that it is desirable to seek at the start some common ground — some point of possible present agreement."

—7ames C. Fernald.

A COURSE IN WRITING PRINTED SALESMANSHIP 6" A COURSE IN SELLING PRINTED SALESMANSHIP o far, I think, we have had impressed upon us S What I might term the great universatility of the INTRODUCTION or APPROACH. As a matter of fact, that procedure is almost instinctive. We Work more surely and accurately, however, for the analyzing and knowing of our instincts.

We have seen advertisements without introductions, and we have, furthermore, been impressed with the element of strength that inhered in them, but we have also seen that such strength came from a radical change of copy; that is, they were not aflrmative but evidential.

By earlier Lessons we have also learned that as a rule evidential copy does not go into periodical space; we occasionally see it there, but not generally.

The one great reason for this, as we have learned, is that periodical space, being expensive, automatically limits the use of space— and evidential copy (in its proving sense, and very frequently in its clear sense) requires space.

We have, indeed, seen these facts working out even in the evidential copy reproduced from periodicals. We have seen that such copy lacked the usual elements of presentation, i.e., Introduction and Conclusion, and we have also seen that Presentation in its rhetorical sense was also lacking; in other words, such copy was, though strong, elemental and crude. Given space, such blemishes would disappear.

So we have seen that periodical copy (when Written right) tends to the affirmative style, the profier of a booklet being the bridge over which the periodical reader is led into the pages of the booklet, where, with ample space, the presentation can be made rhetorically and exhaustively.

We can accordingly rank the INTRODUCTION or APPROACH as one of the great principles of advertising-selling procedure and such positive examples as have been given ought to be suficient to guide the student in that direction.

Errors can be made in INTRODUCTION, however; we see a type of such error in the announcement of the ELGIN WATOI-I. This is all INTRODUCTION and no PRESENTATION. Art is there, an appeal to the historical and philosophical is there, and one is led to the watch —— and left there.

Examine the announcement as a stranger to the Elgin Watch and you will see the sales appeal is so very meager that the announcement is literally starved for it. We find the watch, of course, and illustrated, but it differs in no material respect from many other watches; we find it guaranteed by "Elgin guarantee," but we have no means of determining whether that is any more advantageous than the guarantee we would get with any other good grade of watch. There is no offer to supply further information if needed; no booklet is oflered; we may be sold on abstract time, but we are not sold on the Elgin Watch — and this because INTRoDUCToRY space has monopolized practically the entire page to the exclusion of PRESENTATION, either in the announcement or in a proffered booklet. A

As a unit in itself, or, in other words, as an isolated announcement, the advertisement fails, the standard of judgment being selling force, or printed salesmanship.

IN writing a business announcement either in advertisement or booklet form one can begin with either INTRODUCTION, PRESENTATION, or CONCLUSION, as the spirit moves; but probably the best procedure for the unskilled is to write the PRESENTATION first, adding INTRODUCTION and CoNcLUsIoN later, because, after all, the important thing is to get down to selling, and that point cannot be arrived at till PRESENTATION is made. It is essential to remember this. Above all, avoid CIRCUMLOCUTION, a term it would be as well to define fully here and now:

"CIRCUIVILOCUTION. Indirect or roundabout expression; the use of many words where few would sufiice; a periphrastic expression; hence, lack of condensation or POINT in speaking or writing. Applied attributively by Dickens to government officers and ofiices, on account of their circuitous and tedious methods.

'How not to do it was the great study and object of all public departments and professional politicians all round the

"Circumlocution is used especially when direct statement is intentionally avoided, as when a suitable term is not at hand, or when a speaker, from delicacy or with a view to soften the force of a direct expression, avoids the use of a single term.

"Syn.: diffuseness, periphrasis, pleonasm, prolixity, redundance, redundancy, surplusage, tautology, tediousness, verbiage, verbosity, Wordiness. CIRCUMLOCUTION and PERIPHRASIS are roundabout ways of expressing thought; CIRcUMLocUTIoN is the more common, PERIPHRASIS the more technical word. Constant CIRCUMLOCUTION produces an affected and heavy style; occasionally, skillful PERIPHRASIS conduces both to beauty and to simplicity. Etymologically, DIFFUSENESS is a scattering, both of words and thought; REDUNDANCY is an overflow. PRoLIxITY goes into endless petty details, without selection or perspective. PLEoNAsM is the expression of an idea already plainly implied; TAUTOLOGY is the restatement in other words of an idea already stated, or a useless repetition of a word or words. 'I saw it with my eyes' is a PLEoNAsM; 'All the members agreed unanimously' is TAUTOLOGY. VERIBAGE is the use of mere words without thought. VERBOSITY and WoRDINEss denote an excess of words in proportion to the thought. TEDIOUSNESS is the sure result of any of these faults of style..4nt..' brevity, compactness, conciseness, condensation, directness, plainness, succinctness, terseness."

From this definition it is plain we should avoid:

Circumlocution. Surplusage.
Dilfuseness. Tediousness.
Pleonasm. Verbiage.
Prolixity. Verbosity.
Redundancy. Wordiness.

We shall make possible exceptions, however, in favor of:

PERIPHRASIS and
TAUTOLOGY,

because the above two terms, it will be plainly seen, have two separate and distinct meanings and are in that sense each really two words.

Note, for instance, the double meaning of TAUTOLOGY, i.e., (I) "A use/ es: repetition of a word or words," and — (2) "The rertatement in other words of an idea already stated."

In the second sense TAUTOLOGY should be used in business literature much more frequently than it is. It is, in that sense, practically a checking up of the reader's thought with a view to being sure that he does not miss the vital point.

PERIPHRASIS, under certain conditions, could really mean the INTRODUCTION, or the extended treatment of the subject in accordance with the requirements of the audience.

I n fact, the AUDIENCE to he reached has ct profound influence on the rhetoric or methods to he employed. In treating a technical subject with a technical audience it would be manifestly foolish to go into an extended explanation of terms, but just such a treatment would be manifestlynecessaryin explaining a technical subject to an audience oflaymen.

In considering CIRCUMLOCUTION, note its antonyms, i.e., brevity, compactness, conciseness, condensation, directness, plainness, succinctness, terseness; and note that the term "SHORT" is avoided. The reason will be plain if we examine the definition of:

"SHORT... 4. Abrupt in mafmer or spirit; curt; cross; as, he was very short with me. 'She answered in accents short, cold, and severe.' — OWEN MEREDITH, Lucile.

N ot reaching or attaining a requirement or result; falling below a certain standard; deficient; inadequate; insufficient; scant; often with of," as, short of the full amount; short weight; short in needed material.... 9. Things that are lacking in quantity, quality, etc."

It will be seen that in steering the Course of Brevity between C1RcuMLocuT1oN and SHORTNEss, considerable judgment is required; they constitute, in fact, the Scylla and Charybdisf of the writing art.

As these Lessons proceed we will find principles that, like instruments, will enable us to avoid wrecking our PRESENTATION craft, and one of the chief factors, as already explained, is to know our audience in the mass, or as a kind of composite picture; the second is to visualize them with the eye of imagination. This will come later.

The term is not fully defined, but extracts given will be sufficient to illustrate the point.

T "CnARYEDIs. (L.) Class. Myth. A ravenous woman, whom Jupiter transformed into a treacherous whirlpool on the Sicilian coast. In attempting to avoid this whirlpool mariners were in danger of the opposite Italian rock Scylla; hence the proverb 'To sail (or to be) between Scylla and Charybdis,' i.e., between dangers or dithculties from opposite sides." — Standard Dictionary.

Before leaving CIROUMLOGUTION we might pause on one of its synonyms, i.e., PLEoNAsM, which, as we have seen, means "The expression of an idea already plainly implied," and it is one of the ironies of business presentation that business men (who err in demanding "Short" copy) will also demand PLEONAsM (which is apt to make it tediously long). '

We will understand this better if we get the meaning of the term "implied" through:

"IMPLICATION. I. The act of implying or de ducing; deduction; also, that which is implied or involved; something properly to be inferred, though not directly stated; a fact or truth involved in some other fact or truth; an inference; as, an IMPLICATION is often more important than the direct statement.

'The law... frequently supplies by its IMPLIcATIoNs the wants of express agreements between the parties.'

— PARsONs, Contracts."

" IMPLICIT. 1. Fairly to be understood, though not specifically stated; tacitly comprised; implied."

To illustrate: Some years ago I was preparing a booklet designed to sell orchard ground in the West. A great volume of proof was at hand evidencing the transfer of land at constantly increasing values, as cited by local newspapers, transfer records, etc., and editorial comment on constantly rising values, remarkable sales, etc. These facts I reproduced literally, naming source of publication or folio of record of transfer, etc., with names of parties concerned both in sale and purchase. On reading these the very obvious IMPLICATICN of any reader not an idiot was that lands were not only enhancing in value very quickly but must continue to enhance in value. My client took the MS. to a friend of his who (of course) got that inference out of it. Then he made a discovery. That fact had n't been written down. The writer had of course been remiss. This indicated a rather curious development. The mind, as it were, doubles back on itself. It gets the inference intended for it to get out of the MS. — and then demands to know Why that inference is n't written down! It thinks it has discovered carelessness or that it has proof that a vital omission has been made! The only thing to do under such circumstances is to explain to the reader that he has committed PLEoNAsM and, if that term does n't awe him, painstakingly to explain just how he came to "discover" what he did — a conclusion that, if correctly explained, is apt to surprise him considerably, because till then he thinks he has seen you miss him, when as a matter of fact his whole attitude and frame of mind reveal that you /zit him.

THERE seems to be no single term in the English language which describes a manuscript that is not a word too short or a word too long, but which is "just right." Such a word or term ought to be invented because it is badly needed. Mr. ames C. Fernald in his work "ExPREs-sIvE

ENOLIsH," under Chapter XVI, dealing with THE ART or BREVITY, seeks to differentiate the distinction by the terms:

MECHANICAL BREVITY and ESSENTIAL BREVITY.

I quote extracts:

" There is a brevity measurable by the clock or by count of words, which may be called MECHANICAL BR1-:vITY. Such brevity is as definite and positive as the figures on the face of a check, and often as obligatory. If six speakers are to have ten minutes each in a meeting of one hour, no one speaker can take more than his ten minutes without defrauding another.. The writer faces a similar requirement under still more imperious rule.

"Physical and mechanical necessities do largely control speaking and writing, however much'we may resent the fact..

"Mechanical brevity has now become, with many persons, an obsession, and in our publications merit is measured by fractions of an inch.... Literature is reduced to one dimension, and its excellence estimated in proportion to its shortness."

Yet —

"Every opinion worth having requires toil and time. Thinking takes time, and the expression of thong/zt in writing or printing requires space."

On the other hand:

" ESSENTIAL BR-:v1TY cannot be measured by the clock or determined by count of words... it says I have strongly recommended purchase of this excellent work, and now repeat that recommendation.

just enough for the occasion, and no more... One who does not think clearly will make a communication brief by leaving out what it is highly important to say.... Brevity when it becomes confusing is not a virtue, but a vice. The good and safe rule is, Never saerifiee elearnesx or force for the Jake of arevily. When in doubt, be explicit. True brevity makes sure of saying that, the saying of which is the only object of speaking or writing at all.

"Brevity is comprehensiveness—according to the derivation the 'grasping together' of the subject, so that the speaker or writer sees the whole at once and all parts in their relations."

Mr. Fernald, it will also be noted, avoids the use of the term "Short" — as a matter of fact the phrase so common to business, "Make it short," literally means to "Make it inadequate; insufiie cient and scant; make it lack in quantity and quality," and the mischievousness of such instructions ought to be apparent enough from what has been said. What is wanted in all business material is ESSENTIAL BREv1"rY——not one more word than should be there —— not one word less than should be there, the measure being that of the Missourian, "Show me," with all the implications and necessitations that the request conveys.

If necessary forget the rhetoric, but remember you have to 5/10-w—completely, and clearly, and interestingly; therefore do not attempt to build ibattleships in back yards, nor fly aeroplanes in theaters.

"Words are but pictures of our thoughts."

—Dryden. "A single little word can strike him dead." — Luther.

"Such are the vicissitudes of the world, through all its parts, that day and night, labor and rest, hurry and retirement, endear each other; such are the changes that keep the mind in action; we desire, we pursue, we obtain, we are satiated; we desire something else and begin a new pursuit." — Yohnson.

" Fair tresses man's imperial race ensnare, And beauty draws us with a single hair."

— Pope.

" Look here, upon this picture, and on this." — Shakespeare.

A COURSE IN WRITING PRINTED SALESMANSHIP 65' A COURSE IN SELLING PRINTED SALESMANSHIP

N a prior lesson I stated:

"So we have seen that periodical copy (when written right) tends to the afi-irmative style, the proffer of a booklet being the bridge over which the periodical reader is led into the pages of the 500/elet, where, with ample space, the presentation can be made rhetorically and exhaustively."

It might be as well to give some attention to this bridge "over which the reader is led" because, as we all know, there are bridges and bridges— some invite us along attractive footpaths in our rural strolls and others turn us back.

The M. DENsIvIoRE (COMPANY advertisement (taken from Motor Boat) oflers a standardized 36foot motor boat; I am ignorant of the price, but from my knowledge of things nautical I would assume it to be between $5000 and $6000.

Men who buy these standardized types of craft are relatively poor— $5000 is a sum that looms large to them and it is not parted with lightly — such a sum will procure such a man a home, or a farm, or many of the hasic things upon which his life rests and revolves.

If he rents a fiat and abandons his hope of a farm to buy a pleasure craft for a home, he is perfectly well aware that he fastens that home to the end of a rope every night and may lose it or find it seriously damaged any stormy morning.

To the type to whom the standardized boats appeal (at between $5000 and $6000) salesmanship of the highest type and class is required.

AND THE " BRIDGE" in this case is a "FoLDER"!

" In this connection procure and peruse "THE BOOKLET — KING or SALEs MEDIA."

Apart from my personal impressions and beliefs (as expressed in "TI-IE BooKLET— KING or SALEs MEDIA ") I maintain that the term "Folder" in connection with a product selling at from $5000 to $6000 is psychologically wrong. It sounds cheap, and, when I come toit, that quotation from Holmes leaps to mind:

"The smallest word has some unguarded spot
And danger lurks in it without:1 dot."

To me this "Bridge" is not inviting; to the layman I do not think it will prove any more inviting than it does to me, although the factors that influence him may be dil-'ferent from the factors that influence me.

When a man expects to consummate one of the dreams of his life, his natural expectation would be to approach it through dignified and adequate media; the BOOK ranks highest in literature; the BOOKLET is "a little book" and ranks highest in sales literature and in buying literature.

There are certain anticipations and expectations we all form in connection with relatively big transactions of our life, and the type of man who proposes to pay out five or six thousand hard-earned dollars for a pleasure craft has the,psychological expectation of approaching it along pleasant literary lines. He may recover from the shock of being tendered a " folder," but it certainly does n't help. Furthermore, the boating industry at the present time is endeavoring to coax people on to the water and in that attempt is meeting the competition of the automobile. The literature put out, therefore, should be highly positive and constructive, both in conception and effect. A "folder" is a bad anticlimax in such case.

IN the BEN. E. ARvIs announcement "The Bridge" is an "Illustrated Circular" (something that has a perilous relationship to the "dodger" in the layman mind) and this is worse than a

"folder."

One likes to enter upon a buying path in a spirit of pleasurable exploration. One likes to feel that beyond the bridge there are further delightful vistas of knowledge and information, and this attitude is rudely checked when the periodical road leads to a "folder" or a "circular."

Nor is the situation much bettered by the oifer of a "catalogue" (see announcement of WIScoNsIN MOTOR Mro. Co.), because_one knows that the average "catalogue" is a dry-as-bones affair, and this somewhat forbidding PICTURE "'

"' We will later see that words or terms arouse corresponding pictures in the mind that can be harsh and repelling, or pleasant and inviting.
held in mind regarding such documents distinctly RETARDS the IMPULSE to send for it. Contrast the warmth of the HARTNIAN invitation to send for catalogue (Lesson No. 16).

The MIssoURI ENGINE COMPANY commands one to send for "Bulletin." The very sense of "Bulletin" arouses a negative impulse, it being:

"A brief oflicial summary, publication, or placard."

In all these cases the "bridge" is of a character to turn one back in lieu of coaxing one forward. There is no suggestion of attractiveness heyond, and there is certainly no improvement in the variation of the AMERICAN ENGINEERING CoMPANY in proffering a "Price List."

HAT we are dwelling on now, it is well to note Wcarefully, is an important psychological principle in advertising. That is, under such conditions we should strive to inject the glamour of the beyond into the prospect's mind, remembering that one of the terms in our definition of "Salesmanship" is "Moving" (Lesson No. 6), always keeping in mind the fact that men tend to move toward attractive situations and away from unattractive ones..

In traveling, the lure is always ahead; it 's the next bend of the road that draws us On; if we are permitted a glimpse of blue hills and lovely valleys there is our incentive, but we lose in great part our desire to proceed further when we come prematurely into the uninviting country of PRIcE.

Now, against the somewhat forbidding examples we have been examining in this Lesson, compare (to change the simile) the warmth and cordiality of the PAcI:ER's TAR SOAP announcement.

"A woman's crowning glory is her hair," and women appreciate that truth intensely. In this announcement (to revert to our original simile) the woman reader is led to a "Bridge" beyond which, very evidently, lies an attractive path of knowledge and information in regard to a subject in which she is vitally interested and through and by which others are delighted and charmed.

PAciER's oPfers to SHOW —— attractively.

The reader is moved on from the publication to the booklet.

We must eventually come to price, but when we do it should be under conditions that satisfy DEsIRE. Price named, or goods offered prior to DEsiRE BEING REAciiED, represent PREMATURE SALEs ATTEMPT.

The LURE begins in the announcement and continues into the SALES DOCUMENT beyond.

It is NOT called a "circular," a "bulletin," a "price list."

The term "Manual" is, in view of the subject and aim, chosen with judgment and discretion, as witness the definition:

"A compact volume; handbook; a compendium con taining the essentials of a subject; elemental text-book; primer."

In the light of contrast it will be seen that:

The tendency of the PACKER announcement is to move the reader on.

The tendency of the others is to halt or rebufl'.

Understand, neither tendency is absolute; every woman will not answer the PACKER announcement; many people will answer the other announcements; but the PACKER announcement removes FRIOTION which the others have. Many gasoline engines can be made to RUN — but some run well, some badly, some indifferently. Advertising is just the same; some announcements creak It should be carefully noted that our critical analysis has gradually changed from tactics of INTRODUCTION to BRIDGE from Introduction to Sales Presentation. From what has gone before it will be understood that if we were considering announcements repro duced in this Lesson As A WHOLE, they would be subject to far more criticism than has been given them.

and groan and lose selling power through friction, nevertheless, like the gasoline engine, they get there; they eat up MONEY like old, worn, or imperfect engines eat up GAS, but they do run."

Engineers study to reduce WASTE and FRICTION and they progress as they find what waste and friction are, and where they are, in mechanical things (physical things). So we will progress as we find what waste and friction are, and where they are, in psychical things.

TI-IE GENERAL SERVICE DEPARTMENT AMERICAN WRITING PAPER COMPANY JOSEPH A. BORDEN, DIRECTOR

IO SOUTH LA SALLE STREET, CHICAGO, ILL.

PUBLISHERS

AMERICAN WRITING PAPER COMPANY

JOSEPH A. BORDEN, DIRECTOR

lo soUTH LA sALLE sTREET, cHIcAG0, ILL.

PUBLISHERS

"Fancy, like the finger of a clock,
Runs the great circuit, and is still at home."

"When my way is too rough for my feet, or too steep for my strength, I get off it to some smooth velvet path which fancy has scattered over with rosebuds of delight; and, having taken a few turns in it, come back strengthened and refreshed." — Sterne.

"Pleasure is a shadow, wealth is vanity,'and power a pageant; but knowledge is ecstatic in enjoyment, perennial in fame, unlimited in space, and infinite in duration. In the performance of its sacred offices, it fears no danger, spares no expense, looks in the volcano, dives into the ocean, perforates the earth, wings» its flight into the skies, explores sea and land, contemplates the distant, examines the minute, comprehends the great, ascends to the sublime — no place too remote for its grasp, no height too exalted for its reach." — De Witt Clinton.

A COURSE IN WRITING PRINTED SALESMANSHIP is' A COURSE IN SELLING PRINTED SALESMANSHIP

AKE the type of advertisement that begins Twith a generality, continues with generalities, ends with generalities, and sends the reader 'out into the wide buying world with a generality for buying guidance — how would you classify it?

It is not logical, for the very essence of logic is to move toward VERIrIcATIoN.

And —-

If it is n't logical, what is it? What is its status?

Consider all that Logic embraces; the celebrated British logician Duns Scotus, who lived in the thirteenth century, called it not alone the Science of Sciences, but also the Art of /1rts.' I

As Jevons points out:

"The very name of logic occurs as part of nearly all the names recently adopted for the sciences, which are often vulgarly called the 'ologies' but are really the 'logics,' the 'o' being only a connecting vowel or part of the previous word. Thus geology is logic applied to explain the formation of the earth's crust, biology is logic applied to the phenomena of life; psychology is logic applied to the nature of the mind; and the same is the case with physiology, entomology, zoology, teratology, morphology, anthropology, theology, ecclesiology,thalattology, and the rest. Each science is thus confessed to be a special logic."

' See Jevons, Locic, page 79.

T Jevons, LEssoNs IN Loorc, page 7.

There is only one answer; when we test the "Generality" type of advertising with logic, we find it is only logical to the extent of the generality. It touches logic there, and there only.

We have seen, on the other hand, that SELLING is, fundamentally, a purely logical process; we must also see that the " Generality" type of advertising touches selling only to the extent of the generality that is a characteristic feature of it. This being the case we have simply swung a great circle of proof and are back at Lesson No. I, with its three circles, with our "Generality" type of advertisement in the middle between the salesman and the writer-salesman..

In other words, the "Generality" type of advertising is, as in Lesson No. 2, "An enfeebled

ERHAPS the reader should be cautioned'here Pto review Lesson No. 20 in the light of all previous lessons. We must not, for instance, suppose that all page advertisements that attempt to sell are forced to use generalities, or that all page advertisements are weakened by generalities. A large proportion are (when the product being sold is intricate, expensive, and highly competitive), but a proportion again may not be; we saw the opposite tendency, for instance, in the EssEx announcement, the WHITE TRUCK announcement, and (most admirably) in the HARTMAN announcement (Lessons 15-16). The double-page advertisement of the Lexington Motor Car Company reproduced

Performance.7 ii On Motor Parkway. Long Island. same ear. without changing carburetor adjustment. 3 reached maximum of 77 miles an hour by speedometer that, according to report from Stewart Company, manufacturers, was IV; miles slow at 60 miles an hour, indicating that actual speed of more than 73% miles an hour was attained. A ll measured mile was covered in 56 seconds. 'Li

ACCELERATION

From one to sixty miles an hour in a distance of 800 feet. all the way in high gear.

GASOLINE ECONOMY

The same car. without changing carburetor adjustment, ran 23. miles on one gallon. oi gasoline. Standard test gasoline was used. the gas tank being filled from Q P; roadside fuel pump. I The foregoing tests were conducted in a stoclt model Lexington car equipped with l ii; an Ansted motor, manufactured by the Lexington 'Motor Co., this being the motor I that won first and second places in the free-for-all Pike's Peal: Hill Climb in Sep-I it' tember. I920. Each and every record above set forth is covered by the sworn.

statement of the oflicial observer. on file with the undersigned company, available

for inspection by the public upon request. So far as we know and believe, this is the first presentation that any motor car concern has ever made of its combinationrecords on the four _vital points covered. As the majority of automobile owners well,

ltnow, a car may be geared down for hill worlr or geared up for speed. but a combination of speed and power to the extent herein recorded is truly phenomenal.

The gasoline economy record, taken in 'conjunction with the foregoing feats on hills and the straightaway, in our opinion, surpasses all records heretofore made and'

will. we believe. stand for many years to come.

COMPANY OF NEW YORK

Bedford Ave., cor. Eastern Parkway, Brooklyn, N. Y.

in this Lesson carries, it will be noted, a strong sales appeal; note also that it furnishes verification as it proceeds.

We find a different type of selling appeal, but nevertheless an undeniably effective one, in THE LOCOMOBILE COMPANY announcement; great inferential deductions can be taken out of this LOCOMOBILE advertisement and each reader will write in his own special message to himself, according to his individual reaction.

The R. C. RATHBONE announcement is a good example of VERISIMILITUDE and its power to bring a point home to the reader with great suggestive sales force.

THE missing element in all these announcements is THE BRIDGE that will take the reader from the publication to the business. In considering this point it must never be forgotten that the bridge which brings the "prospect" to the advertiser can be later used to ta/re the advertiser to the "prospect."

This fact, with all its implications, is so stark and obvious and elemental that one can but marvel at those who do not seem to see it.

It means so much, it counts so tremendously, it makes such a startling difference, not alone at the beginning, but with the progress of time.

Take automobile advertising merely to illustrate the point. I am a New Yorker and impressed with the EssEx announcement (Lesson 15). At that time it makes the EssEx loom up like a great mountain to me; but I am not ready

Damages.111/1111..., 11.. 1.. 1..1...... ... 1...... 1..1111....1..... ,...1.........1. 1.. 1...... 1..........1. 1.. 11... . 1.1....1-1.. 1...1 11...1-11. 11.11......1. 1111...1. 1.1-. 1...1 B h r 11-1.1.1' 1'.'1. "1.1....'.11 1. 1...11.....;...1..;..1...1. 1v-- :1-1-re---e iwfl "W ""'"" ' ""''=', §'.'. . E1.".1, 1.11..1'..Z'1T.§h'1'.1..,';2. 11. ... 1.51151'.........1........-1... '.=';.-1.-::- ;.:'.::1. 2:...-.:.'."..'z-..'".".w.-::'=-M.1... --»»»=-4 1»-..'..-1-..:.':1."-.::-..':§§.'":. :1:11:11 j..1.11.... 11. 1:11.-11 1-..111. 1¢.11y 1.1. W n::_1.'.r.."11-1., 11$'.'. 1;::..M1.:,._".n._1.:1:b'1 M,,, M,_,,",_ "HM m M 1...... 1......11..1..11 11.1.... 1. ...111.-,,,,.,_ c,,,,,,,_,,,,,,_,___, ___,_, m 1... . 1.......1§.1...1. 11.... 1..,4,1-@111-1 1.. 11 1.14. 1... "M111-.11 11. Imund "M ' F" MI '4 '"""-"" 11-w¢. Mm 1 M-'.'"-'- ""...1.1..........1...1......1.1.1 1...

Bloodjood. 11.1 11.. Pnyne n111.1u-. 1111.11.1-1...... 111111.. 1:111-1.1111. »---' _ _ _ __ 1:'.-1.':-'.'.'..'1.:..":'.'.... ..1 "-1-J" '-lid In wurl I 1... numay 11 would he vlncvd n A 11.1-1 nldum X, lwo nl 11: W'lb1lEl'Il nl Inn': -.........1 1...1. 11.......1..1. 1.........1.......1. 1.....1. 11....

The Skid.-ling Seuon is Always Productive of Expensive Accidenll A11.1. n1.y11¢s=y...1....1.=.y...1r1»...1.11..... 1..1....i:.11m....11&i.¢v¢1.

and unkind Animtyou in not oonly. I-'er insuna:

When $5.000/ 10.000 com M00 $60,000/100,000 would cvfl only $43 additional

B1'AlLl8H@ I853

R. C. RATHBONE 8: SON llcurjoflkl

INSURANCE BROKERS

TELEPHONE so LANE Cubic Addrco 4:30 JOHN New Yak "1z..11..1., u. Y1" to buy at that moment; so time gets in its leveling work; other things demand my attention and the ESSEX points are gradually erased from mind.

In time, as I come to an automobile purchase, the newest and strongest presentation naturally impresses me more than that of an older day UNLESS my first impression has been REINFORCED by a series of other impressions.

It might be contended here that the continuous advertising of the Essex takes care of this, but, if I recollect aright, I took the Essex announcement from a publication I only OCCASIONALLY read, and it is easily possible that the announcement in turn was in a publication the Essex people only OCCASIONALLY used.

It might indeed be possible that an Essex account, EXPERIMENTING with certain media, continuously engages in a process of ELIMINATION, so that the media used today would not be used a year hence (it might, for instance, have been found unprofitable or unsuitable), yet that might be the medium I would read continuously, hence there would be another failure to "connect" there (assuming the "Follow Up by Advertisement" theory was being followed).

This is a very wide and important angle of our subject and we cannot follow it out here in all its conclusions and implications, but they are tremendous. For instance, it may happen that an automobile company wants to make a private announcement to its customers and prospective customers; it does n't know t/zem, and it ha: n't got them, how can it? It is then forced to use all past media (probably at great expense) to ensure reaching all past readers. Its proposed PRIVATE announcement then becomes PUBLIC. We can easily conceive conditions where that might be very embarrassing—the era of price recessions through which the industry has passed, as an example. A public announcement immediately "posts" all competitors, overnight. Under some commercial conditions "the psychological moment" is suflicient if it endures over forty-eight hours. But it will not endure for that period if blazoned into publicity in public sheets.

Then consider an automobile company cultivating, developing, and bringing to the "prospect" point hundreds of thousands of people literally in the dark, because it does not know them individually and only guesses that "out there somewhere" a future buying constituency is being formed. Is it any wonder that bankers refuse to consider such forms of advertising as "credits" for loans?

We have realized how THE BRIDGE and THE BOOKLET (for illustrative example see Packer Tar Soap announcement, Lesson No. 19) bring the "prospect" out of the dark, out ofspace, out of the unknown, to the advertiser, over the Midge he lays when he ofiers an attractive booklet in form that STIMULATES a budding customer to reveal himself.

Immediately (under correct business tactics) this name with its address is seized, crystallized on records (3 X5 cards usually), and becomes a potential asset to the advertiser.

In course of time he has thousands or hundreds of thousands of such "potentials" — not some where out in space, BUT ON RECORD, in his files. Now, at definite times and periods, or at psychological moments that he will know best how to utilize, HE can Go BACK over his advertising "Bridge" to those "potentials" again. He can, at decisive moments, troop his salesmen to those people in regiments of hundreds if necessary, and he can throw out PRINTED SALESMEN to those people in troops of thousands, or hundreds of thousands if necessary; he can strike, once, twice, thrice, or a hundred times if necessary.

If he has laid his bridge well, very nearly every one in whose breast flamed the slightest or faintest interest is on his record: (not somewhere out in space, unknown, unreachable, and lost) and his market is beneath his hands, known, recorded, classified, indexed, and available, direct (not through the attempted expensive intermediary of publications used in the past, that, otherwise, he might not wish for various reasons to use again).

Contrast this with the plight of a manufacturer who, while knowing that "somewhere out there" are hundreds of thousands favorably impressed with his product, still cannot reach them when he wants to in the way that he wants to, and (if his unbridged advertising has extended over some years) cannot reach a large proportion at all, no matter what method he adopts, even though, in the attempt to do so, he may retrace his advertising steps into all publications used in the past and revive his advertising in them at terrific expense.

The difference is as the difference of the poles; the difference between the known and the un known; the diflrerence between the light and the dark; the difference between the realizable and the unrealizable; the "bridge" advertiser has specific, concrete, determinable things to work on, while the other has just the opposite.

The advertiser who ignores "bridging" tactics in his advertising announcements deliberately flouts all the tremendous potentialities wrapped up in Allocation, Location, Cultivation, Culmination, Repetition, Accession, etc.

And he also flout: one of the most productive tools of business — THE FoLLoW UP.

BUT even assuming that a manufacturer does not want to "Follow Up" — —even assuming that he does not want to be " bothered" with oflice salesmanship — even assuming that he prefers to lean on publications exclusively T to do his selling work —assuming that his business is sufiiciently big and profitable to offset such enormous waste as must inevitably accrue, still will any manufacturer deny the value of having potential customers RECORDED, even if the records lie dead and inactive? There may come times, and there do come times, in the history of all business enterprises when such names and addresses become supremely important to have, and of great value to have, not alone positively, but negatively— in other words, the ability to reach "potentials" DIRECT (with a two-cent stamp) may save hunu0w UP" (Consumer booklet) and "Pnmn:n Snu-:snumsm1" should be read in conjunction with this lesson. _ _ T " STRIKING THE NORM IN ADVERTISING" should be perused in this connection.

dreds of thousands of dollars at a crisis when those hundreds of thousands may be vitally needed.

An excellent "Bridge" to coax those who need» better heat,from periodical to advertiser, with roadbed back from advertiser to reader at any time business exigencies call for it.

AMERICAN WRITING PAPER COMPANY
JOSEPH A. aonnzu, nnu=.c"ron
IO sown LA SALLE STREET, cmcmo, ILL.
PUBLISHERS

"There is no danger in the nine—volume philosophical encyclopedia, but watch out for the pamphlet that fits in the side pocket and sells for a few sous. " —— Voltaire.

" Fortune! There is no fortune; all is trial, or punishment, or recompense, or foresight." —— Voltaire.

"The way of fortune is like the Milky Way in the sky, which is a meeting or knot of a number.

of small stars, not seen asunder, but giving light together; so are there a number of little and scarce discerned virtues, or rather faculties and customs, that make men fortunate." —— Bacon.

"Thoughts there are that need no embodying, no form, no expression. It is enough to hint at them vaguely; a Word, and they are heard and seen." joubert.

A COURSE IN WRITING PRINTED SALESMANSHIP 6-' A COURSE IN SELLING PRINTED SALESMANSHIP

N reviewing "Bridgeless" advertising as exemplified I in Lesson No. 21 (LOCOMOBILE, RATHBONE), it might be contended that such advertisers, making a specific point at a time, would ultimately "cover" their Presentation with the same force as a booklet. In other words, a complete presentation would ultimately be made if the points of the product were explained point by point over a period of time, in a series of advertisements, one being practically continued into the other.

This, to be sure, is an excellent way of advertising, and it is to be highly recommended and endorsed. Nevertheless, it does not dispense with the necessity of either THE BRIDGE or THE BOOKLET. It would if the audience could be gathered together and kept together while the series runs, and if that audience, starting from the status of possibilities (all at one time), could be converted, first to "prospects" and secondly to buyers or customers, all at one time.

Human nature is n't like that, however; some buyers come at the first few shakes of the business tree. Others, still ripening, refuse to fall till they have been ripened fully. Some men who give way early in the discourse will be found among any audience, while others require the final words of Conclusion, Recapitulation and Peroration before they are convinced. One advertisement may bring a section of readers to the buying point, two advertisements influence a second section, three influence a third, four convert a fourth, and so on.

. When the "prospect" is at the buying point, the psychological moment has arrived to close him, and at that moment he should be able to cross the bridge, get the booklet, absorb the complete st0ry—and buy.

Therefore a series of advertisements, each making a specific appeal, should, in each series, present the selling booklet for examination and acceptance at the moment the " urge" is felt.

Properly speaking, the advertisements should spring from and base on BOOKLET, this insuring logical AGREEMENT between context in PERIODICAL selling the INQUIRY and context of BOOKLET making the SALE. I do not mean by this that advertisements should be literal reproductions of booklet text, but I do mean

'that the booklet text should inspire them.

Business is a constantly moving and essentially roaming and restless proposition, however, and it sometimes happens that a series of advertisements ultimately forms a booklet, or suggests basic material for a booklet. It is better to arrive at the booklet by this process than not to arrive at it at all, but as a great general rule the BOOKLET should be prepared before advertising, because in the great majority of cases advertising is functioning wastefully without the booklet.

In other words, the moment publicity gets to work it is ("somewhere out there," as it were) shaping men up into "prospects" and we want methods and principles that stimulate those "prospects" to register their favorable reaction with the advertiser. That, of course, means BRIDGE and BOOKLET.

Later we may find it advisable to ACCENTUATE and STIMULATE the first favorable reaction which those "Prospects" advised us of, and then we utilize the

BRIDGE we laid for them to come to us in sueh fashion that we go to them.

WHEN we examine the advertising situation we find that a large proportion of advertisers are leaning too heavily on their PERIODICALS for SA1.Es. A thousand horse-power is driving their "INQUIRY" department, with ten horse-power functioning on SALES. This is another side of a very important factor that can only be touched on lightly here, but one phase of this error is seen in the BRIDGELESS, UNSUPPORTED, ASSERTIVE advertising that drives possible "prospects"1' to all sorts and conditions and kinds of dealers, distributors, representatives, etc., there to be handled tactfully or untactfully, with knowledge or without knowledge, with skill or without skill, as CHANCE elects.I

As a matter of fact, the great majority of "BRIDGE1.1=.ss" advertisers are, by general statements (to which conditions force them), sending "prospects" into the general market, there to be handled and molded and converted as chance or fate serves; the best that can be said of such tactics is that the who/e husiness is heing stimulated and out of this general stimulation each gets his share.

This in itself would not be a bad consummation provided each got an equal and ratable share, but we know from observation that many get a starvation allowance which eventually sends them into bankruptcy.§

Should not truth, evidence, accuracy, specificness, concreteness, begin with the manufacturer, and not

' The error and futility of this will be apparent after a perusal of "PRINTED SALESMANSHIP." 1' All advertising has same selling force (see Lesson N0. 2). See "Tm: MASTER SALi:sMAN." Note incident of "Six Little Tailors" in booklets 2-3 of "I3Un.omo A Pxmrmo Busim-Lss." have to be sought in the generalized market? By all rules of logic it should, and all rules of logic are manifestly violated when it does not.

The prospective buyer should go into the general market primed with unassailaa/e facts furnished to him by the manufacturer.

But how can this be done when manufacturers' , tactics seem deliberately planned so as NoT to con nect? How can a man be made a FRIEND who is deliberately held at arms' length by the very nature of the periodical announcement?

Do you not see the terrible folly of it all? Can you not sense at least the frightful wastes that are as a consequence taking place? Do you not begin to see how the long record of insolvencies and receiverships rolls up? Do you not see that "advertising" is on its apex in lieu of its base?

NOTHER side of the PERIODICAL error will become A apparent if we examine THE TREATMENT or INQUIRIES as they are received by many manufacturers who provide the bridge.

The fact of the matter is that manufacturers as a whole lean too heavily on PERIODICALS for results, not realizing (and perhaps under many conditions literally not caring) that PERIODICAL effort and DIRECT OFFICE or DIRECT-MAIL eflort should run abreast if the maximum of business wished for is to be procured.

Personally I feel that every dollar spent for periodical work should be matched by a dollar spent for OFFICE SALES WORK. I feel that if $100,000 is spent annually on PERIODICALS (that, by and large, and in the main, simply produce POTENTIAL business), another $100,000 should be spent on SALEs ORGANIZATION, SALES MANAGEMENT, PRINTED SALEsMANsi-iii, LETTERS, BOOKLETS, etc., and I believe it is only ignorance or carelessness that prevents this.

And I say, if only $100,000 is available, that such a sum should be deliberately "split" to the end that each PERIODICAL "Inquiry-Producing" Dollar should be matched by an OFFICE SALES-PRODUCING DOLLAR. Till this is done the ratio of SALEs MADE in proportion to INQUIRIES REcE1vED will always be abnormally low. In "The Follow Up" I have cited a manufacturer who "Sells" a ratio of two out of every five inquiries received, and while this ratio could not be accepted as a standard to which all lines could conform, it is nevertheless true that the percentage of SAi.Es to INQUIRIES in all lines is ENORMOUSLY SMALLER than what it should rightfully be.

If manufacturers will realize that, in a very large sense, periodicals are merely INQUIRY-PRODUCERS, and that their OFFICE must be a SALES-CENTER, and a SALES-PRODUCER,'l' Advertising-selling will take a long leap forward. Further, this realization would not HURT the PERIODICALS. It would HELP them, because, under different methods, PERIODICAL advertising would produce far better results.

INQUIRIES are the SEEDS from which spring SALEs. The SEEDs must be GERMINATED and CuLT1vATEi)1 by the SALES DEPARTMENT, otherwise they will grow wild and thin and straggly, as wild things do.

' When conditions competitively are practically equal (as regards quality and rice), this is a very clear demonstration of ineffective SALES Woizi—an object esson in the unerring working of CAusE and EFFECT.

1' Veritably "Tan MAs'rEn-SALi:sMAN." _ _ I The very definitions of the terms " Gern-iinate" and " Cultivate " are highly suggestive, as witness: _. _ "GEiunNATE. To begin to... develop into a higher form. " _ "CuL'i'ivATE. To improve or develop by study or training. To pay assiduous attention to."

Every organization should be a master salesman.

Selling force should generate at headquarters.

It should never be delegated or handed to jobbers or wholesalers, dealers or distributors, salesmen or representatives, branch or "chain houses," or county, state, or district managers.

ALwAYs, the ORGANIZATIoN should be the PARAMOUNT salesman, AccEPTING such MEED of SALEsMANSI-IIP as its STAFF tenders, ACCEPTING the Co6iERATIoN or THAT STAFF, and INsPIRING IT TO Co6PERATIoN, but ALwAYs it should be GREATER than its DISTRIBUTING FAcT0Rs, greater than its AivERTIsING, and MEAsURE UP TO ITS FULL STATUS AND RESPONSIBILITY AS MANAGER, DIRECTOR, ORGANIZER, AND MAsTER or SALEs.

ALwAYs, the ORGANIZATION should be in DIRECT ToucH with its "Potentials," its "Prospects," and its "Market." Its staff of distributors and representatives and salesmen and advertising men may also be in touch, but they should always work under the MAsTER HAND, and within the KINGDoM of the ORGANIZATION. IT SHOULD SELL ITS DISTRIBUTORS, SELL ITs SALEsMEN, SELL ITS AGENcIEs, and, ABOVE ALL, SELL ITs CUSTOMERS.

ITs REcoRDs SHOULD NoT LIE "OUT IN THE DARK" either among a PERIODICAL clientele, a DEALER clientele, or a SALEsMAN's clientele, but be under its hand, as an asset, in its own files.

IN SHQRT, THE ORGANIZATIQN SHOULD OWN ITS BusINEss IN EVERY SENsE IN WHICH THAT STATEMENT CAN BE INTERPRETED.

Perhaps a simple illustration will make this clearer: On the opposite page we find four circles; the outermost is

THE BUsINEss, embracing WITHIN IT its DISTRIBUTIVE and SELLING activities as represented by

WHOLESALERS AND J-OBBERS, DISTRIBUTORS AND DEALERs, and GENERAL REPRESENTATIVES, who in turn embrace or environ "PoT1-:NT1A1.s" and "CusToMERs" — simply a logical illustration of the LARGER CoNTA1NING THE LEss.

The conditions outlined by the circles are violated by bridgeless, generalized, and assertive advertising, because the whole tendency is against causing the "potential" to register himself at headquarters, with

' "ENVIRON. To be or extend round; enclose; surround; encompass; as, the city was envinmed with a wall.

" 'The great function of envinmment is not to modify but to sustain.' — DRUM

MOND, Natural Law." —Slandani Dictionary.

the record of attention, interest (and probably desire), that his inquiry would automatically carry.

Under such circumstances, of the great army a portion remain silent, quiescent, unknown; another portion (with buying instinct aroused) register (in person or by inquiry) with dealers or representatives (who have no dovetailing arrangements or system with HEADQUARTERS); another portion, under influence of the same instinct, seek THE GENERAL MARKET (as along Automobile Row, New York), there to be roped in by competitive distributors and representatives of rival houses.

Under more logical tactics, as embraced in BRIDGING, SPECIFIC, AFrIR1vIATIvE, AND EVIDENTIAL processes, the greater part of the great army reached would MANIFEST itself, REGISTER at HEADQUARTERS, and become ACCESSIBLE FROM HEADQUARTERs for such GERMINATION and CULTIVATION as were called for.

In greatly enhanced returns the difference in concept and strategy would justify itself thousands of times over.

ALI. the above verges on BUsINEss ANALYSIS rather than business writing, or the art of writing printed salesmanship; nevertheless it will be seen that the latter art bears an exceedingly close relation to ANALYsIs, SYNI'IIEsIs, and PERIQDICAI. advertising; in truth, BAsIC PRINCIPLES of WRITTEN SALESMANSHIP cannot be grasped without a working knowledge of these related arts; just as the physician must possess a working SURGICAL knowledge, and the medical or surgical SPECIAI.IsT possess a general knowledge of both medicine and surgery, so must the WRITER-SAI.Es-MAN possess a general knowledge of the PRINCIPLES that lie beneath all Advertising-Selling efiort.

We are dealing now, it may be said, with Fmsr PRINCIPLES of Advertising-Selling, and from these we will rise (if limitations permit) to secondary or subsidiary principles, but all that is being said gives CI.Ews to enormously more that MIGHT BE said. Think, therefore, along these lines, and as you think you will see almost illimitable angles and facades of the subject; as you see them, "PRINT THEM — MAIL THEM." Advertising is a rudimentary science, as yet in an almost formless stage, and to form it, shape it, direct it aright, and to keep it in true relations and proportions to its various parts and activities, is something that requires all the brain, all the versatility, all the personality, all the thought and talent and genius we can UNITEDLY control or command; it is literally work for MEN, and for a great army of men such as the TYPOTHETAE membership represents; it is a CAUSE we can throw ourselves into heart and soul because it is assuredly a great and worthy one.

Conditions today show PERIODICAL ADVERTISING dominant as to ATTENTION, MANAGEMENT, EXPRESsIoN, and EXPENDITURES. That condition is logically and provably wrong—— a lesson that is to be taught to hundreds of thousands, and that it will as a consequence require thousands of men to teach; spread the true word, therefore, by word of mouth, by letter, by booklet, by house organ; prove the true word as you go by citation, exemplification, and illustration; stand on reason and demonstrate by reason.

ADVERTISING-SELLING is apparently the best form of selling because it is simplified to the last degree for the advertiser. All he has to do is to sign a contract for three, six, or twelve months as the case may be, hand his data to an advertising agency, and periodi cally mail checks. In "general" advertising, indeed, the procedure is reduced to the last degree of simplicity because inquirers and buyers alike are not invited to correspond or get in touch with headquarters, but are thrown, more or less indirectly, into the hands of wholesalers, jobbers, retailers, representatives, etc.

As far as "General" advertising is concerned, therefore, the advertiser is but an animated pocketbook for agency and publisher. This condition varies, of course, more or less in degree, but it undeniably rules more or less in such circumstances. It is in one sense not the publisher's fault, nor the advertiser's fault, nor the agency's fault.

All are taking the line of least resistance and all are gomg "the easiest way. "

But it is not the best way. IfI have failed to show that, I have indeed failed. Dimly, reluctantly, all classes concerned are beginning to wake up to the situation. The publisher finds it more difficult to maintain the ratio of advertising he must have. The agencies find it more difiicult to open new accounts and to keep older accounts. Manufacturers complain constantly of " the high cost of doing business."

Despite all handicaps, despite all friction, despite all carelessness and indifiference, despite all ignorance, the PERIODICALS, attractively edited, and with enormous circulations, frequently take up the heterogeneous load and deliver it. That is, through sheer force of wonderful circulation, they make advertiser and agency succeed in spite of all. Stupendous publicity will take a particle of salesmanship, a fraction of selling force, and " put it over" because it magnifies it to such infinite proportions.

But this condition docs not rule universally either; all advertisers are not making good; all advertisers are not making profits; there is a continuous mortality.

An analysis of one great periodical (full-page advertisers being considered only) gave 997 concerns advertising from Jan. 6, I917, to Oct. 15, I921, inclusive.

Out of a total of 943 concerns, 664 stopped full-page advertising before January 1, 1921—a seventy per cent "mortality" or "death rate."

Unless publishers, agencies, and advertisers alike face facts like these, all are going to suffer.

I maintain that the CAUSES which produce these EFFEcTs reveal themselves clearly and thoroughly under proper analytical treatment. I maintain that written selling has exact, inexorable, logical LAws, and when those laws are observed, the EFFECT is success, just as, when they are violated, the EFFEcT is failure.

HE advertiser who does not want to run an appal ling risk in his advertising ventures will, among other things, establish a sound sales mechanism behind his advertising mechanism.

This does not say (this can hardly be emphasized too much) that pure periodical advertising does not make sales. It does. Therein, indeed, is the subtle and misleading factor that runs to ruin and disappointment. It would really be better if it made no sales. Each advertiser would then recognize the necessity for AN ADvERTis1No DEPARTMENT and A SALEs DEPARTMENT, each of equal efiiciency.

Mr. Smith, in his insistence on THE Bus1NEss being THE MAsTER SALEsMAN (see "THE MAsTER SALEsMAN"), has gone to the foundational elements of the situation. The business, at headquarters, should hold

' I cannot do better than refer back to Lesson No. 2.

the reins and drive and guide and handle, and interpret and understand all the complex factors with which it is dealing. Its attitude should be P0s1TIvE, not NEGATIVE. It should, throughout, SELL To (distributors, representatives, public), and not be sold for. No jobber should dominate it; its "potentials" (in which is wrapped its good will) should not lie scattered in hundreds of distributors' hands, or inert, "out there, in the dark." Its IMPRESSIONS when made, should base so solidly, firmly, and irrefragably on fact, truth, proof, and evidence, that boast and claim and assertion would be as the water against the steel prow of a great ocean craft. Surely plain, simple truth must shine out of the mass of words through which I have reached this situation. It is a great subject, and I have but vaguely outlined it, yet sufiiciently perhaps to encourage others to explore further; to probe further, to illustrate further, and to bring their versatility, talent, and genius to it.

It would be fitting if printed salesmanship came into its own through the printing craft.

And why should it not? Behind us is all the might of right. I have spun no tenuous theory. Truth rests on proof and reason rests on fact; we can trace back by INDUCTION or forward by DEDUCTION, we can go from principles to cases, or from cases to principles, and ever our answer is the same, and ever the note rings true — our cause is RIGHT.

Forward it then BY THE PRINTED Wom), that mighty power that has ever led the world from darkness to light!

(This concludes settion N0. 2 of our Course and the relation of the subject to periodical advertising.)

A COURSE IN WRITING PRINTED SALESMANSHIP 6-' A COURSE IN SELLING PRINTED SALESMANSHIP

From DEPARTMENT or GENERAL SERvicE AMERICAN WRITING PAPER CO. Jos. A. Borden, Dirzctor IO SOUTH LA SALLE STREET

AMERICAN WRITING PAPER COMPANY

_osI-:II-I A. BORDEN, DIRECTOR

Io SOUTH LA SALLE STREET, CHICAGO, ILL.

PUBLISHERS

"Neither rain nor snow nor heat nor gloom of night stay these couriers from the swift completion of their appointed rounds." (Carved in stone facade of New York Post Office.) —— Attributed to Herodotus.

"The post is the grand connecting link of all transactions, of all negotiations." — Voltaire.

"A stray volume of real life in the daily package of the postman."

— Douglas Yerrold.

"The value of a principle is the number of things it will explain." —Emerson.

"The productions of the press, fast as steam can make and carry them, go abroad through all the land, silent as snowflakes, but potent as thunder. It is an additional tongue of steam and lightning, by which a man speaks his first thought, his instant argument or grievance, to millions in a day." — Chapin.

A COURSE IN WRITING PRINTED SALESMANSHIP 63-' A COURSE IN SELLING PRINTED SALESMANSHIP

WHEN we look at periodical advertising We see that advertisers therein regard readers of these periodicals as "possibilities" and not as "prospects" for their goods (or services). These are two terms adopted more or less by business, and it might be well if we defined them right here so that we will understand them fairly well whenever they are mentioned again.

"POSSIBILITY. I. The fact or state of being possible; often implying improbability; as, a porribility of life. 2. A possible thing; that which may arise or take place; something that lies within the reach of power to efl'ect;... a contingency proximate or remote."

"PROSPECT. 1. An indication justifying hope or expectation, especially of good; a future probability based on present indications; as, a youth with bright prorpectr.... 2. (Commercial Cant, U. S.) A prospective buyer."

Put in terms of business understanding, it may be said that a "Possibility" is some one you mail to or advertise to in the hope that a responre will be made (indicating interest).

Till such a person does so respond he remains "a possibility." When he does respond he becomes, in the business vernacular, "a prospect." If he buys he becomes a customer.

The periodical advertiser does not bother about the readers of a periodical in which he advertises till they respond to his announcements;

' Referring, of course, to newspaper and magazine announcements.

then they become "prospects" to him, and (if his business is conducted right) their names and addresses go in records, or on 3 x5 cards, to be filed in due course in alphabetical, chronological, geographical, or other order, to be "Followed up" (after being attended to in the first instance) in due course by letters, booklets, house organ, or other media, or by salesmen, or by dealers.

I-IE important point to be noted above is that men and women advertised to remain "possibilities" till some of them by acts of their own (by inquiry) automatically announce themselves as "Prospects."

The average advertiser in a newspaper or magazine, in other words, would not, if he could, buy or otherwise obtain the subscription list and consider it of any great value to him; he is only interested in that proportion of the subscription list that replies to his announcement.

This seems like common sense and it is common sense. A man can advertise bicycles, for instance, in a newspaper of one hundred thousand circulation, but all experience teaches him it would be foolish to expect to find one hundred thousand buyers of bicycles comprising that circulation. He knows that will not be so, and he only values that small proportion of such readers which reveal themselves as probable buyers of bicycles, by inquiring about them, because why would any one inquire about a bicycle that had no interest (direct or indirect) in a bicycle? The answer of course is that no one does, and consequently inquiries only come from those who have an interest (direct aor indirect, remote or intense, as the case may be) in bicycles. And of course that holds true of all other commodities or services.

' The various file manufacturers (such as the Globe-Wernicke Company) publish extensive literature on filing and card index systems which should be procured if the reader has not a working knowledge of that branch of business.

It also of course holds true of BOOKLETS offered to periodical subscribers (whose ultimate design is to get such subscribers as write for it to buy what the advertiser ofiers in said booklet). Take, for instance, the L. . MUELLER FURNACE Co.'s booklet (Lesson 21). It is not for a moment to be assumed that all subscribers of the Saturday Evening Post (in which the announcement appeared) will want that booklet; only a proportion will, and that proportion will be of value to the L. Mueller Company becausethey have revealed (by inquiry) that more or less directly or intensely they are interested in heating appliances; in other words, these inquirers (though a large number will not be sold) will be good "prospects, " and, as "prospects," will be sent the booklet and (in all probability) carefully "Followed up."

I want to make this ADvERTIsING principle very clear and distinct; it is, I hope, understood that THE LIsT which the PERIODICAL goes to is only a list of "Possibilities" in the advertiser's eyes. He only values it as a possible list CoNTAINING the "Prospects" he really wants. What he is after, basically, out 0/' that list, are the "redhot" PRosPEcTs.

Such an advertiser, using a paper of say one hundred thousand circulation, would not want to buy its subscription list, and, regarding its subscribers as "prospects," send them all a booklet without request, and follow them up without invitation or encouragement or indication that they were interested. There might be only a thousand people out of that hundred thousand interested in what he had, and you can see for yourself that if he were foolish enough to assume one hundred thousand were interested, and mail them on that assumption, certainly he would lose a considerable sum of money, because the profits on the thousand he might sell to would be swallowed up in paying the postage, printing, and labor expenses involved in mailing to the hundred thousand.

Yet this very thing is very frequently done in DIRECT-MAIL advertising.

Let us illustrate with a man starting up in business. He has something to sell by mail, let us say, priced at $10. He wishes to conduct his campaign by mail; having no "prospects" he goes to a list broker and procures a "list" of names and addresses of people who are likely buyers of what he has to ofier.

Prior to this he has prepared a booklet; this, we will say, is a complete selling document, with order blanks, etc., enclosed. All those on the list have to do on receipt of it is to read and order.

' Men who buy names and addresses from business firms to sell to other business firms, as, a firm selling books may sell its list of book buyers eventually to a list broker who will resell the list to some firm selling other books.

As a great rule the result of mailing under such conditions will be a'loss. Some sales may be made, but the profits on those will be swallowed up by the general mailing cost.

Such a man, partly informed, may have heard of the "Follow Up" and, to get properly started and to retrieve his original loss, "Follows up."

As a great rule, the result will be a further loss. Some sales will be made, but the profits on these will be swallowed up in the general mailing cost.

As a great rule, the more a man tries to do 'business under such conditions, the greater his loss will be; and the greater his courage, and the greater his perseverance, the greater will his loss become.

This is because the man is violating the law of INTEREsT —— and ATTENTIoN. This law is so unerring in its effects that an expensive fiasco can almost always be predicted when it is violated.

I will cite briefly a few typical cases from my own observation:

No.1. Casualty company. Offering attractive automobile policy. List of automobile owners circularized with an expensive folder. Result, almost a total loss.

No.2. Patent medicine company. List

of patent medicine consumers (over a hundred thousand) circularized on a proposition in which it was judged they would be interested. Result, total sales of less than $5; loss, heavy.

No. 3. Investment ofering. Elaborate and expensive brochure mailed to some ten thousand investors. Result, a loss of $4500 on the mailing.

Let me repeat, these are typical of a large numher of cases I have run across, directly and indirectly, which show that a SELLING DocuMENT mailed DIRECT, without the preliminary of securing an INQUIRY FOR IT, almost INVARIABLY FAILs.

If one will think carefully it will be seen that what is n't a good thing for the periodical advertiser to do is n't a good thing for the DIRECTMAIL advertiser to do.

The periodical advertiser does n't MAIL to the whole list he advertises to—he only mails to that proportion of the list which answers his advertisement.

He procures those ANswi-:Rs—not by presenting a sales proposition (usually), but by a preliminary "canvass" of readers by a brief announcement which (if answered) paves the way for a bigger SALES DOCUMENT.

HE DIRECT-MAIL advertiser, though he Tdoes n't perhaps use periodicals, follows the same PRINCIPLE. He buys or compiles such a list as he can secure of people wholly or partly interested. These are his "possioilities," just as the readers of a periodical (the subscription list) are the advertisers'. "possibilities." To these "possibilities" he sends out one or more letters.

I define these letters as "Inquiry-Bringing" or "Canvassing" letters, it being their intent and province to canvass the list of "possibilities" and stimulate inquiries from such proportion of that list as may be remotely or intensely INTERESTED.

In this connection and relation such letters are the periodicals or newspapers of the DIRECTMAIL world, and the MESSAGE in them stands

"_ It will be un_derstoo_d that we are engaged now with selling to the general public. Special and technical selling tactics will be taken up later.

equivalent to the ADVERTISEMENT of the periodical or newspaper world.

These "Canvassing" or "Inquiry-Bringing" LETTERS may be as infinite and as versatile in their APPROACH as "INQUIRY-BRINGING" or " CANvAss1No " odvertz'sements.

Such LETTERS are ADVERTISEMENTS IN LETTER FORM (Inquiry-bringing, Canvassing, or"Bridging" advertisements) or, if you want to reverse the illustration, such ADVERTISEMENTS are practically LETTERS in ADVERTISING form.

You begin to see here, perhaps, how ADVERTISING principles and DIRECT-MAIL principles dovetail and interlock and how it is not much good to make a study of one unless you also make a study of the other.

THE number of "Inquiry-Bringing" Letters to be sent out to a specified "List" varies with: (A) The price at which the product is being sold.

(B) The margin of profit per sale..

(C) The cost of duplicating the list.

Generally speaking, a small-priced article, with a relatively small profit (something, say, selling at a dollar), will limit (per list) number of "Inquiry-Bringers" and extent of "Follow Up."

Such a proposition may, for instance, work with one inquiry bringer an "Answering Letter" and Booklet (or other enclosure) and three "Follow Ups." There is no fixed ratio to be observed in these matters, and responses and profits must _ ' For examples of which see "Bridging" or "Booklet" advertisements reviewed in past Lessons.

determine what can be permanently adopted. If (after experiment) it is seen that "Answering Letter and Booklet" get the bulk of the orders, and that ensuing "Follow Up" is n't profitable, then that "Follow Up" can be dropped, for there is the answer.

Elements have come into the above, as follows:

(2) "Answering" Letter (not yet defined). (3) Booklet (afairworking knowledge assumed, that we will add to later). (4) "Follow Up" (Ditto). (5) Lists (Ditto).

While the "Inquiry-Bringing" Letter differs in some degree from the "Inquiry-Bringing" advertisement, the dilierence is not so great as to prevent recognition of a common principle in each. Take, for instance, the NUoL advertisement (Lesson No. I4.) and we see it has the essentials of a LETTER: '

Mr. John Doe, Kairn, Iowa.

Dear Sir: Over 750,000 people will die in the United States this year from preventable disease, etc....

Will you not test NUJOL for yourself? Your nearest druggist can supply you. Cordially yours,

Nujoi. LABORATORIES,

By

' The reader is cautioned that advertising rules are full of exceptions, and each case has to be interpreted specifically, in the light of general knowledge. It sometimes pays to open initial accounts at a lass (as is done with "Leaders," for example), the sale of one line leading to the sale of another.

A printed blank in the above letter could make it easy to send for booklet "Dangers of Constipation."

The NATIONAL SALEsMEN's TRAINING AssocIATION advertisement is just as adaptable:

Mr. John Doe, Kairn, Iowa.

Dear Sir: When a_man steps from a $50 a month job as a farmhand to a position that pays him $1000 the very first month— is it luck?...

Think what it has been worth to others to send for the facts. It can be worth that much or more to you. Will you not mail the enclosed blank to-day? There is no obligation incurred. Sincerely,

NATIONAL SALEsMEN's TRAINING AssociATIoN,

BALTIMORE AND OHIo or U. S. SHIPPING BoARD advertisements, with relatively slight changes, could be transferred into excellent "Inquiry-Bringing" Letters; the same is true of the PELTON advertisement (all in Lesson No. I6) and of others that have been illustrated throughout the fore going lessons.

THE "Answering" letter, as its name implies, is theletter answering the inquiry after it is made. Usually a booklet either accompanies it or is mailed simultaneously with it under separate cover.

The phrasing of the "Answering" letter varies greatly in accordance with the special circum

' The LETTER thus becoming, like the advertisement, a combination " Sales Letter" and "Inquiry-Bringer" — a very efiective amalgamation at times. If you wish tobecome a good letter writer, watch the advertisements of firms out lo sell. Such constitute constant object lessons, available at all times in the pages of t_he magazines.

l' It will, of course, be understood that I am merely taking opening and closing sentences to illustrate the point being discussed. stances and conditions governing each proposition, but it should be remembered that its province is to help make the sale, and that, in many cases, it arrives at the psychological moment to make the sale, not alone because a large proportion of "prospects" will be "half sold" and in the mood to buy, but also because it will have the full weight Qf the booklet behind it.

The "Answering" Letter and Booklet, therefore, constitute the big gun of the campaign.

The letter may wish to accentuate one special point in the booklet that, above all, the "prospect" should not miss.

It may wish to summarize the booklet for the busy business man.

It may wish to interject an "emotional" appeal.

It may, in short, wish to do any one of many things, and if it is a "form" or "processed" letter careful thought should be given to its subject matter.

In many instances (particularly where the expenditure is high) it is best personally dictated, or intelligently guided in varied appeal (through "choice of forms), by a high-grade correspondent.

All these subjects will naturally and automatically develop further as these lesson proceed.

' "Passion and emotion... may be always treated as thought in a glow." — Marlineau.

In other words, all so-called "emotional" copy bases an thought, or reason, or intellect, notwithstanding the assertions of those who evidently never think the matter through to a conclusion.

s a great rule, any worth-while campaign will A be composed of the following units of " copy ": (I) Display advertisements (probably "Inquiry-Bringers"). (2) Classified advertisements (probably "Inquiry-Bringers"). (3) "Inquiry-Brin ing" or "Canvassing" Letters. (4) "Answering" fetter. (5) Booklet. (6) Follow Up. (7) Enclosures for "Follow Up."

We will consider these in the order given: (I) DISPLAY ADVERTISEMENTS Many illustrations have been given in these lessons. Other illustrations may be constantly seen in magazines. The rules formulated in prior lessons should guide in preparing these. The "copy" should be dflirmatioe or Evidentiol, or both, and should "Bridge" the gap between

Periodical and Business in accordance with ways illustrated previously.

Display advertising (or indeed any advertising) may not be any part of a proposed campaign. It may be elected to conduct it solely through the mails. I embrace it because lesson students should be prepared to write this type of "copy" if called upon to do so. It will probably be found best to charge for-writing the copy but to let a regular "placing" advertising agency insert in periodicals chosen, do periodical checking, etc.

Advertising (as it relates to checking up copy to see that insertions are made, that right position has been given, etc.) is a business in itself, and the printer may find himself in an unnecessary complication if he assumes it. A "checking" or "placing" agency, as a rule, "carries" the account for the advertiser, and has specialized information in regard to circulation and character of periodicals that is of value. I believe "Advertising" (as utilizing periodicals) and DIRECT-MAIL (as advertising media) should fall into two separate, specialized, and individualized activities or forces, each good in its place, and each closely related and coordinated, one with the other, and I believe the day will come when each activity, recognizing its special functions, and its special faculties and abilities, will separate; this means that a clear, sharp line of demarcation will be drawn between them (as between physician and surgeon). Indeed, the whole "drift" is in that direction. There is already a differentiation between "DIRECT-MAIL" and "AD-vERTIsING." The agency of the future will specialize in placing messages in right mediums (factors of circulation, character of readers, etc., being closely analyzed); it will carry accounts, it will check insertions, etc. '

It may develop a-special faculty for "Inquiry-
Bringing" copy also.

Minds of that type will coalesce in "AGENCY"
work and will represent ADVERTISING minds.

Selling minds will by the same token gradually DETACH from "AGENCY" work, and coalesce with "DIRECT-MAIL" afliliations, WRITER-SAI.Es-MEN, etc.

Advertising space, as a great rule, is not selling space (because cost limits it so sharply), but INQUIRY-BRINGING space.

' The distinction drawn between the advertising mind and the selling mind in "PR1N'rED SAI.EsM.ANsm:P" should be carelully noted.

"We love to expect, and when expectation is disappointed or gratified we want to be again expecting." — 0hns0n.

"No heart is empty of the humor of curiosity, the beggar being as attentive in his station to an improvement of knowledge as the prince." — 0550?"

"Ethics is the science of human duty. Arithmetic tells man how to count his money; ethics how he should acquire it, whether by honesty or fraud. Geography is a map of the world; ethics is a beautiful map of duty. This ethics is not Christianity, it is not even religion; but it is the sister of religion, because the path of duty is in full harmony, as to quality and direction, with the path of God."

— Professor Swing.

"To live is not to live for one's self alone; let us help one another." — Menander.

A COURSE IN WRITING PRINTED SALESMANSHIP 9A COURSE IN SELLING PRINTED SALESMANSHIP

WE were on Display Advertising at the close of Lesson No. 23, and we have dealt with this at sufiicient length for the time being, except perhaps to say this, which marks a vital difference between "Display" and "Classified," i.e. —

The periodical reader seeks classified advertising.

Display advertising see/es the reader.

The distinction, psychologically, is important, and it should be kept in mind; in brief terms we might make a further distinction by stating that classified advertisingi (on the whole) caters to a need, while display advertising (on the whole) seeks to create a need.

In selling, the claims of "Classified" advertising should not be overlooked. The "Business Opportunities" column (or classification), together with "Financial" and "Real Estate," ol¥ers publicity at a very low price, of the most practical and frequently very satisfactory kind.

Itrust it will be understood that when I use the term "periodical" I refer to advertising media — i.e., newspapers, Weeklies, magazines, etc.

T I assume it would be largely superfluous to explain what classified advertising is; the "want" columns will suggest themselves to every newspaper reader.

A good many advertising agencies issue booklets or other media giving rates and lists of " classified" media (chiefly, the great daily newspapers, and particularly their Sunday editions), and these should be procured and kept on file.

REVIEWING Lesson No. 23 again, I believe it desirable to reémphasize and restate an important sentence that occurred within it, i.e.—

A selling document mailed direct, without the preliminary of securing an inquiry for it, almost invariably fails.

I sincerely hope that I will be able to burn this fact (or principle) into the mentality of every reader of these lessons to such effect that he will never, consciously or unconsciously, make the mistake of mailing (or allowing his customer or client to mail) a booklet (or other selling media) till the person it has been designed to sell to has EXPRESSED A WISH To RECEIVE IT.

A customer comes in to you; he has, over a number of years, acquired, say, ten thousand names on his mailing list; he has been converted to a booklet and "follow up" and Wants to make that list productive.

If left to his own devices he will probably order ten thousand booklets (that being the total of his mailing list), and, when you deliver them, mail them to those ten thousand names. The result will probably be a flat failure; that is, there will be a disappointing dearth of results.

Now, perhaps that customer is a "sport" who can take a licking with a smile, and he grits his teeth and says, "Very well, I did n't perhaps hit them hard enough, so I 'll put in a 'Follow Up.'" So he comes to you again, and maybe orders a "Follow Up" of twelve letters, with perhaps twelve enclosures, in sets of ten thousand each, which he mails out — to experience another flat failure.

Probably he does n't get as far as the twelfth letter before he washes his hands of "advertising" and declares in no uncertain tones that he 's "through" with it forever. Why shouldn't he be, under such conditions? The more he spends, very apparently the less he makes, and he has only to continue along the same road for a sulficiently long period to drain his resources. Naturally he stops. Your printing presses stop to the extent of that one man also.

Furthermore, the man has a tongue and voices his experiences. That does n't help printing any.

I commented on this recently as follows:

"A letter is really nothing more or less than a little newspaper or periodical with its circulation controlled by its sponsor; it gives what the newspaper gives—— space for a message. The resultfulness or otherwise of that space depends (as in the newspaper or periodical) on the extent of the circulation it is given, among the right kind ofpeople, with the right kind of message.

"As a rule, a business story, when interestingly and convincingly told, is far too long for the single issue of space that either a newspaper or a letter can give. In that event the proper procedure is to tell the business story in a booklet and then tell the public to be reached (by advertisement or letter) that you have a business story of interest and value to them that you would be glad to mail on request.

"The man who is interested replies; the man who is not interested does not reply. Hence your letter acts as a sieve that separates interested from uninterested people; hence when your hooklet goes forward in answer to requests which the preliminary letter or advertisement has stimulated, it is sure of an interested audience.

"A great many business men mailing out their booklets without evidence of preliminary interest are eloquently talking to empty benches. They have mailed to ten thousand people, say, and imagine ten thousand people are reading what they mail. As a matter of fact, perhaps not a hundred are reading it—— this is one of the great wastes of mail advertising.

"The man who is advertising correctly is the man who conserves his booklet for interested people; these people are his 'prospects.' The booklet sent out on their inquiry makes customers of some of them. A well-planned 'follow up' makes customers of many more of them. A well-designed mail campaign will have the following units, therefore:

"(I) An 'inquiry-bringing' or 'canvassing' letter or advertisement.

" (2) A booklet with which to answer inquiries.

" (3) A sales letter to accompany the booklet.

I think we learned this lesson pretty thoroughly through foregoing lessons and examples of advertising—we now have to learn as thoroughly that the same principle applies in DIRECT—

MAIL work. As a great rule Ir is CONSTANTLY VIOLATEI) THERE, hence my anxiety to correct that typical error.

"(4) A 'Follow up' (with enclosures) comprising from six to twelve letters mailed from three to fourteen days apart.

"... The mail advertiser (usually) with a specialty to sell (say, for illustration, a machine for more efficiently mowing lawns) first compiles a list of possible buyers. As these are only possihle buyers we will term them 'Possibilities.' He then prepares a voluminous booklet, has ten thousand copies printed, and mails these to the ten thousand names on his list. He gets some orders—not as many as he would like, however.

"... He"follows up' the booklet with a series of six letters and enclosures, getting some more business—not much, but some. He feels 'the high cost of doing business.' What is his error?

"He has taken for granted an interest that did not exist; he has talked eloquently to empty benches; he has considered 'possibilities' as ' prospects.'

"If you have a ball and throw it at a man who does n't request it and does n't know it is coming, he will dodge it—and probably either want to have you arrested or to punch your head. If you throw the ball at his request and with his knowledge, he will try hard to catch it. i

"It takes two to make a buying game, and the attitude of the party of the second part makes all the difference in the world.

sand booklets, costing say ten cents each, to ten thousand people; his postage per booklet has been tvso

WE will call our man Smith;he has mailed ten thou-, cents, and hislabor may be reckoned in terms of two cents more. His total cost, therefore, is fourteen cents per booklet, multiplied ten thousand times, or, in all, $1400.

"He then sends six follow ups, which we can estimate at five cents apiece, making thirty cents for the six, with a total of $3000 for this item. His expense has been, in all, $4400.

" ow suppose Smith had canvassed his 'possibilities' with a 'canvassing' or 'inquiry-bringing' letter. "This 'inquiry-bringer' going to the entire list of 'possibilities' would cost, say, five cents per letter, or oo. $5 "PLAN 'B'

" Say ten per cent of these 'possibilities' indicated , their interest by inquiring, giving Smith a list of 'pros pects ' totaling one thousand to whom his booklets would be mailed.

"One thousand booklets at I4 cents cost him... $140 " His six 'follow ups' at 30 cents (to one thousand 'prospects') cost.................... 300 "His expense has been...................... $940 "And:

"He had nine thousand booklets on his shelves." In other words, the wrong process (Plan "A") cost him $4-4-oo, and the right process (Plan "B") but $94.0. Further, by the right rocess he has nine thousand booklets on his shelves, to the good, or further campaigning, representing (at ten cents each) a further credit or gain of $900. By the wrong process (Plan "A") he would have exhausted these booklets, and would be faced with the necessity of a re-order, which, at cost given, would mean a new obligation of $1000.

T once arises the question of results (in this A illustration it is not necessary to go into illustrative results). VVould they have been greater on the ten thousand mailing of booklets to "Possibilities" (as per Plan "A") than they would be on the "canvassing" of "Possibilities" by "inquiry-bringer" and subsequent mailing to one thousand interested people (as illustrated in Plan "B")?

Out of the business experiences of thirty years I can answer emphatically in favor of Plan "B"; that is the correct method to follow, always, and beyond a doubt. Any number of times in my business experience, firms I have been connected with have been approached by people about to undertake extensive mailing campaigns, and, while preliminary negotiations have been pending I have ascertained what they intended to do, i.e., if they intended to follow out Plan "A." Almost always that was their intention. It almost always is. Sometimes negotiations. ultimately put these people under our guidance and counsel, and other times they tackled their sales problem without our aid. In all cases that I can remember, where they acted for themselves, they perpetrated the error outlined in plan "A," with disastrous results to their plans.

and themselves.

As a great rule the booklet mailed without invitation is not regarded as a guest and will receive an exceedingly cold or indifierent reception on arrival. Remember, we are speaking of attempted sales to the public as represented by a list of "Possibilities." Under such circumstances. the attempt is almost invariably disastrous. Other conceivable circumstances may conduce to a better reception. Almost invariably, however, it is Wrong to mail out a booklet without previously paving the way for it, and without previously arousing desire for it (as expressed in request to send).

THERE are two elements in this situation that present a somewhat dangerous position to printers.

First —The customer (present or prospective) is very likely (knowing no better) to assume that Plan "A" is the correct plan.

Having (for instance) a list of ten thousand names he wants 'to do business with, he is very likely to order ten thousand booklets.

Second—The printer, through a larger order for booklets, will profit by the customer's ignorance or error.

(It will be evident that if the printer explains the situation, a smaller order for booklets will result.)

DO not believe that we need pause long over this situation. Immediate profit is not permanent profit. Every farsighted and conscientious printer wants to establish a customer who will consume printing, rapidly and legitimately, in business transactions in which he is making a profit.

The success of the printer's business is bound up in the success of his customer's business.

Any apparent loss involved in a lesser number of booklets being ordered will be richly balanced by a greater number of other printed things that will be needed as business normally and legitimately develops for the customer.

Under constructive, creative tactics in the spirit of these les sons, customer and printer grow together.

Furthermore, though his first booklet order may be less, a sustaining and growing business ensures continuous orders.

Every Direct-Mail success Helps printing.

Every Direct-Mail failure Hurts printing.

A failure hurts printing in general, and the printer in particular.

The printers' outlook on these things must not alone be broad, but also ethical.

As ethical as that of the physician who works to bring a man back to health by the shortest, most direct, and least expensive route to the patient.

" NGWLEDGE," said the great Bacon, "is

K power." "I repeat," said the great Disraeli,.. that all power is a trust; that we are accountahle for its exercise."

"If you master this great power of advertisingselling (or Printed Salesmanship), you can use it positively or negatively, for good or_for harm, to make the world better or to make the world worse, to lift men up or to throw them-down.

See that you use it right. This refers, not alone to your client, but to those your client goes to. If the cause is not right, if the truth is not there, leave it alone.

PERSONALLY, I have never experienced any difiiculty in getting a client to adopt Plan " B " after the psychology of it had been explained to him.

It may happen, however, that some men will hold that it is better to mail under Plan "A."

In such case, suggest a compromise; suggest that (assuming the list is ten thousand) the list be halved,—five thousand being mailed to under Plan "A" and five thousand under Plan "B" (returns, both in inquiries and ultimate remittances, being rendered traceable by different colored blanks or other "keying" devices).

This will give an object lesson both to client and yourself in favor of Plan "B."

In the meantime look around, question, try to get knowledge of mailings similar to "A" and see if they have not proved exceedingly unfruitful and disappointing.

CPSIA information can be obtained at www.ICGtesting.com
Printed in the USA
BVOW02s1000260214

346082BV00009B/207/P